Ladies aid society

The Good Cheer Cook Book

Ladies aid society

The Good Cheer Cook Book

ISBN/EAN: 9783744792493

Printed in Europe, USA, Canada, Australia, Japan

Cover: Foto ©Andreas Hilbeck / pixelio.de

More available books at **www.hansebooks.com**

THE

Good Cheer Cook Book

BY

THE LADIES AID SOCIETY,

OF THE

EPISCOPAL CHURCH,

CHIPPEWA FALLS, WISCONSIN.

"It is arrant folly, all this quibbling and quiddling over the final cause of our race and the true object of life. Nature has indicated this so plainly that he is the blindest of fools who cannot understand. There is but one theory to which Nature holds the human race inflexibly and that is eating. She forgives neglect of everything but of food and sauce. She forces man to eat that he may live. She plainly intends that he shall live, that he may eat."

HERALD PRINT,
CHIPPEWA FALLS, WISCONSIN.
1889.

WE

DEDICATE

THIS COOK BOOK

TO.

Old House-Keepers

AND

When the daily cry rings through the household,

" WHAT SHALL WE HAVE FOR DINNER ?"

WE

HOPE THEY MAY FIND AN ANSWER
IN THESE PAGES.

" Now, good digestion wait on appetite, and health on both."

PREFACE.

IN sending this Book out upon the "tender mercies" of the world, we do not claim perfection, neither do we intend it as a primary department for those new in the art of cooking, but rather look to the veterans in the culinary ranks for appreciation and support.

During long years of work for church and charity, when all other resources have failed to reimburse our depleted treasury, a good, well-cooked dinner or supper has never failed to bring us in money and compliments.

This knowledge has given us courage to publish our receipts in book form.

Good Cooking Pays. A well-cooked meal will often do more missionary work in a hearty, restless family, than a dozen lectures. This volume contains the receipts we have used for years, with a few more from friends and acquaintances.

They are to us as old friends—the "tried and true"—for they have all been well tested.

They have figured at County Fairs, Bazaars, Banquets, Lunches, Charity Balls, Dinners, Suppers, etc., etc., and are now our paying mine from which we frequently declare a dividend.

We send them forth as a white milestone on the pathway leading us to success in our past efforts, looking to the sale of this Book for greater success in all works of charity for the future.

LADIES OF THE AID SOCIETY,

Chippewa Falls, Wis.

NOTICE.

The figures before a receipt do not indicate that one receipt is any better than another, but are merely placed before them for convenience in reference.

Here is bread which strengthens man's heart,
And therefore called the staff of life.

—PSALM CIV.

YEAST, BREAD, ROLLS, GEMS, ETC.

YEAST.

Always use the best flour, always sift it; use fresh yeast; never forget the salt. Spend all the time and strength you can upon the kneading of the bread, and your bread will be good and light.

POTATO YEAST—No. 1.

Ten large grated potatoes, one quart of boiling water, two tablespoonfuls of salt, one-half cupful of sugar, one small handful of hops boiled in a quart of water, strain the hop water into the other mixture, boil hard five minutes; when cool, add one yeast cake or a cupful of good yeast.

MRS. L. C. STANLEY.

POTATO YEAST—No. 2.

One cupful of hops in two quarts of hot water. Put on the stove to boil; while boiling, grate six large potatoes, add one cupful of sugar, one-half cupful of salt, one tablespoonful of ginger, strain the boiling hop water on the mixture, stirring all the time until it thickens, let it boil up once or twice; remove from the fire, and when cool (not cold), add a generous cupful of good yeast; after rising twenty-four hours, put away in a cool place in a stone jar.

Mrs. A. S. Stiles.

POTATO YEAST—No. 3.

Four large potatoes, pare, boil and mash them, add four tablespoonfuls of white sugar, one tablespoonful of ginger, one tablespoonful of salt and two cupfuls of flour; pour over this mixture one and one-half pints of boiling water, and beat the ingredients until all the lumps disappear; when cool, add a cupful of good yeast; when light, put in stone or glass jars and keep in a cool place.   Mrs. A. J. Cady.

Rockford, Ill.

BROWN BREAD, BISCUITS, ETC.

If you have a small family, or wish to have your brown bread look very pretty, and appetizing, steam it in *one pound baking powder cans.* The slices are then a pretty and convenient size to cut on table or before sending to the table. Every housekeeper has a quantity of these cans about the premises. If your family is small, one of these little loaves is just the thing you need, for brown bread is never good cold, and loses its best points when steamed over.

BROWN BREAD—No. 1.

One and one-half cupfuls of corn meal, one cupful of flour (wheat), one-half cupful of graham flour, one cupful of sweet milk, one cupful of sour milk, one-half cupful of molasses, two eggs, a little salt, one teaspoon-

ful of soda, steam three hours or set the pail containing the mixture in a kettle of cold water, and after it
begins to boil do not let it cease boiling for three hours.

Mrs. H. H. Todd.

BROWN BREAD—No. 2 (Celebrated).

Three cupfuls of sour milk, three-quarter cupful of
molasses, three cupfuls of corn meal. 1 cupful of wheat
flour, one-half cupful of graham, two teaspoonfuls of
saleratus. a little salt ; steam three and one-half hours.

Mrs. A. S. Stiles.

BROWN BREAD—No. 3.

One cupful of sweet milk, two of sour, three of corn
meal, two cupfuls of wheat flour, one cupful of molasses,
one teaspoonful of soda; steam three hours.

Mrs. F. C. Webb.

BROWN BREAD—No. 4.

Two cupfuls of sweet milk, one of sour, one cupful
of molasses, one cupful of wheat flour, one of graham,
one heaping cupful of corn meal, two teaspoonfuls of
soda, one of salt; steam four hours.

Mrs. W. R. Hoyt.

BISCUIT (Raised)—No. 2.

One quart of warm milk, one-half cupful of yeast,
flour to make a stiff batter, two eggs beaten light, piece
of butter size of an egg, one-half cupful of sugar; mix
up stiff and set to rise second time; make out into
biscuit, and when light again, bake.

Mrs. Pische,
Eau Claire, Wis.

BROWN CORN BREAD (Raised).

Two cupfuls of corn meal scalded with enough boiling water to wet through thoroughly, one-half cupful of New Orleans molasses; when cool add one and one-half cupfuls of hop yeast bread sponge and a little salt; stir and put to rise; when light add wheat flour enough to knead in a loaf: let it rise again and bake an hour and a quarter.   DEWAYNE GILBERT.

BISCUIT (Raised)—No. 1.

Scald one pint of sweet milk, add butter the size of an egg ; let it cool, then add one teacupful of yeast. Put two quarts of flour in a dish, pour the milk, yeast and butter in the center of the flour and let it stand over night, without stirring any of the flour in. Next morning stir enough of the flour in to make a sponge; when light, mix in the rest of the flour and more if needed to knead into a loaf: when light again, make into biscuit.
MRS. H. H. TODD.

BOSTON BROWN BREAD.

One cupful of rye meal, one of fine corn meal, one-half cupful of flour, one teaspoonful of salt, one-half teaspoonful of soda, one-third cupful of molasses, one and one-half of sweet milk : steam three hours.
MILWAUKEE COOKING SCHOOL.

BAKING POWDER BISCUIT.

One quart of flour, three heaping teaspoonfuls of baking powder, one even teaspoonful of salt; sift all together five or six times, then rub two tablespoonfuls of butter thoroughly into the flour; mix very soft with milk or water (milk is the best), knead as little as possible; roll out and bake in a quick oven.

Mrs. A. Hoffman.

COLEMAN BANNOCK.

One quart of milk, one pint of corn meal, one-half pint of flour, three eggs, two teaspoonfuls of baking powder, one of salt, one tablespoonful of butter, two of sugar, bake half an hour.

Mrs. Washington Coleman,

Bay City, Mich.

CORN MEAL PUFFS.

Four tablespoonfuls of corn meal scalded soft, one large spoonful of butter put cold in the hot meal, one coffee cupful of flour, two eggs beaten well, one scant cupful of milk, a little salt. Bake in gem tins twenty-five minutes.

Miss Hattie Whitney,

Green Bay, Wis.

FRENCH ROLLS.

One quart of flour, four tablespoonfuls shortening, four tablespoonfuls of sugar, one cupful of sweet milk, two-thirds cupful of yeast. Mix the sponge in the morning, and when light, make it into a loaf: let it rise and about two hours before using, roll out about half an inch thick, cut in three inch squares, butter, and turn over three cornered: let them rise and bake a light brown. These are very nice.

Mrs. T. M. Cary.

GRAHAM BREAD—No. 1.

Two and one-half cupfuls of sour milk, one cupful of brown sugar, or a little molasses, four cupfuls of graham flour, two cupfuls of white flour, two teaspoonfuls of soda, a little salt; this makes two loaves. Steam one hour.   Mrs. W. G. Yates,

Cleveland, Ohio.

GRAHAM BREAD—No. 2.

Three cupfuls of sour milk, one-half cupful of brown sugar, two teaspoonfuls of soda, one-half cupful of wheat flour, add graham flour until you can stir conveniently with a spoon : bake as soon as mixed.

Mrs. A. S. Stiles.

GRAHAM BREAD—No. 3.

One pint of warm milk, two-thirds cupful of yeast, teaspoonful of salt, flour enough to make a sponge; let it rise over night; in the morning, add two well-beaten eggs and a little sugar, stir in graham flour until you have a thick batter; put in two tins; let it rise again; bake slowly.   Mrs. A. Hoffman.

GRAHAM GEMS—No. 1.

Two cupfuls of sour milk, two tablespoonfuls of brown sugar, a little salt, two even spoonfuls of soda, graham flour to make a medium stiff batter.

Mrs. W. R. Hoyt.

GRAHAM GEMS—No. 2.

One pint of sweet milk, one egg well-beaten, a little salt, graham flour stirred in until the batter will drop from the spoon nicely, heat and butter the gem-pans before dropping in the dough; bake in a hot oven twenty minutes.   Mrs. A. S. Stiles.

GRAHAM GEMS—No. 3.

One cupful of graham flour, one cupful of wheat flour, two tablespoonfuls of sugar, a little salt, one cupful of sweet milk, one egg beaten well, two teaspoonfuls of baking powder; bake in a hot oven twenty minutes.

Mrs. E. Seymour.

JOHNNY CAKE—No. 1.

One egg, one and one-half cupfuls of sour milk, one-half cupful of flour, one-fourth cupful of shortening, one-fourth cupful of sugar, one teaspoonful of soda, a little salt, one and one-half cupfuls of corn meal.

Mrs. J. Rumsey.

JOHNNY CAKE—No. 2.

One cupful of sour milk, one-half cupful of cream, one-fourth cupful of sugar, one egg, one teaspoonful of soda, a little salt, corn meal to make a medium stiff batter.

Mrs. J. M. Bingham.

JOHNNY CAKE—No. 3.

Two cupfuls of corn meal, one cupful of wheat flour, three eggs, two and one-half cupfuls of sour milk, one tablespoonful of melted lard, two of white sugar (if you like it sweet), one teaspoonful of soda, one teaspoonful of salt; beat the whites and yolks separately, put the soda into the dry flour and meal and wet up gradually with the milk; add the other ingredients, and lastly the whites of the eggs; beat very thoroughly; bake in a quick oven.

Mrs. Geo. C. Ginty.

MILK BREAD.

One pint scalded milk, one tablespoonful each of butter and sugar, one-half cupful of yeast, stir in three cupfuls of flour, beat well, let it stand three hours, add three cupfuls more of flour, knead again thoroughly, let it rise, make into loaves and when light bake.

MUFFINS--NO. 1.

One pint flour, one cupful of sweet milk, one egg, three tablespoonfuls of sugar, three of butter, three even teaspoonfuls of baking powder.

Mrs. V. W. Bayless,
Minneapolis, Minn.

MUFFINS—No. 2.

One pint sweet milk, three tablespoonfuls of melted butter, one teaspoonful of salt, three of baking powder, flour for a medium batter.   Mrs. J. Rumsey.

MUFFINS—No. 3.

One cupful of sweet milk, two tablespoonfuls of melted butter, two eggs, two tablespoonfuls of corn meal, one and one-fourth cupfuls of flour, two teaspoonfuls of baking powder; bake in gem tins.

Mrs. T. J. Cunningham.

MUFFINS—No. 4.

One pint of sweet milk, three eggs, one cupful of flour, a little salt.   Miss Belle Walrath.

OAT MEAL GEMS.

One cupful of oat meal, soaked in water, one cupful of sour milk, one cupful of wheat flour, one teaspoonful of soda; bake in hot gem tins.

Mrs. R. D. Whittemore.

OAT MEAL BREAD (Celebrated).

Cook oat meal mush the same as for the table, use

about a quart after it is cooked, add a piece of butter the size of an egg, two tablespoonfuls of sugar, and mix at noon. At night, put in three tablespoonfuls of yeast and flour as stiff as you can stir with a spoon; before you leave it for the night, stir in more flour. In the morning *do not knead* but form into loaves, let it rise, and just before you bake it put butter over the top.

Mrs. MARY RICHARDSON.

PARKER HOUSE ROLLS.

Rub one-half tablespoonful of butter and the same of lard into two quarts of sifted flour, make a hole or well in the middle of the flour, pour in one pint of cold boiled milk, one-half cupful of yeast, one-fourth cupful of sugar and a little salt. Do not stir but let it stand over night. Next morning, stir up, knead and let rise until near tea-time; roll out and cut with biscuit cutter. Put a little melted butter on one-half, and lap nearly over the other half. Place about three-fourths of an inch apart in the pan, and bake quickly.

PUFFET.

Three teacupfuls of flour; butter, size of an egg, one and one-half teacupfuls of sugar, two teaspoonfuls of cream of tartar. Rub all together; add one teacupful of sweet milk, one teaspoonful of soda, two eggs. Bake in a flat tin or pie plate. To be eaten warm for tea.

Mrs. A. J. CADY.

RYE BREAD.

Set it as you do wheat bread, using wheat flour; mix as stiff as you can get it with rye meal, add cara-

way seed and a good pinch of salt, knead it well and
bake when light.   Mrs. Himmelsbach.

SALT RISING BREAD (By request).

Yeast. Put tablespoonful of corn meal in a cup, pour
over it half cupful of hot scalded sweet milk, and set it
in a warm place to rise (if it can be kept warm during the night, set the evening before; if not, mix in the
early morning), take one-half pint of warm water in
pint bowl, half teaspoonful of salt, thicken with flour,
about like cake batter, stir in the yeast, let rise an
hour, have ready a pan of flour. For two medium-
sized loaves, take one pint of warm water (if water is
hot, without scalding the flour, the better the bread
will be), stir water into the flour with the above prepara-
tions, beat well, but do not make too thick; sprinkle
with flour, cover and set in a warm place to rise; when
light, mix as little as possible and form into smooth
loaves; have the tins half-full; when risen to the
top it is ready to bake. If your oven is just right, it
will bake in half an hour. Mrs. Mary Richardson.

SODA SCONES (Scotch).

Two breakfast cupfuls of flour, half teaspoonful of
salt, half teaspoonful of tartaric acid, three teaspoonfuls
carbonate of soda. Mix all these things with a large
breakfast cupful of buttermilk. Put large handful of
flour on board, roll paste upon it; sprinkle flour on
top and roll out one-half inch thick. Put on a hot
griddle and bake each side five minutes, after cutting
into square or circular pieces.
                    Miss Christie McDougall.

WAFFLES—No. 1.

One quart of flour, two coffee cupfuls of sweet milk, rub two teaspoonfuls of butter and two of baking powder into the flour, add a teaspoonful of salt, beat the yolks of four eggs very light and mix with the milk, next add the flour, and lastly the whites of the eggs which have been beaten to a stiff froth.

Mrs. F. C. Webb.

WAFFLES—No. 2.

One pint of milk, three tablespoonfuls of butter, a teaspoonful of salt, three teaspoonfuls of baking powder. Make your batter a little thicker than for pancakes.

Mrs. J. Rumsey.

WAFFLES—No. 3.

One pint of sour milk, three tablespoonfuls of melted butter, three eggs, one teaspoonful of soda, a little salt, flour to make a batter little thicker than for griddlecakes. Mrs. A. S. Stiles.

WHOLE WHEAT BREAD.

One pint of milk, scalded and cooled, two tablespoonfuls of sugar, one teaspoonful of salt, one-half cupful of yeast, five cupfuls of whole wheat flour.

WHEAT GEMS.

Mix one teaspoonful of baking powder and a little salt in one pint of flour, add one cupful of sweet milk, a piece of butter half the size of an egg, the yolks of two eggs, well beaten, and lastly the whites of the eggs beaten to a stiff froth. Bake at once in a quick oven.

Mrs. F. C. Webb.

MEMORANDA.

MEMORANDA.

Ephraim is a cake not turned.
—HOSEA, CHAP. VII.

GRIDDLE CAKES, FRITTERS, MUSH, ETC.

GRIDDLE CAKES.

BUCKWHEAT CAKES—No. 1.

Pour boiling water over one-half cupful of corn meal, put this in two cupfuls each of flour and buckwheat, mix with a quart of warm water, add one-half cupful of yeast, beat hard ten minutes; set to rise in a warm place. In the morning, beat well and set to rise again before you bake them. Save a coffee cupful of batter for the next morning, when you will have to add a teaspoonful of soda.

MISS HATTIE WHITNEY.

BUCKWHEAT CAKES—No. 2.

Warm one pint of sweet milk and one pint of water, put half of this mixture in a stone crock, add five teacupfuls of buckwheat flour, beat until smooth, add the rest of the milk and water and a teacupful of yeast. Some put in a cupful of wheat flour.

MISS S. A. MELCHING.

BREAD CRUMB PANCAKES.

One pint stale bread crumbs (not dried), one pint of scalded milk, one tablespoonful of butter; pour the hot milk over the crumbs, add the butter, and soak over night; rub through a squash strainer and add two eggs, one cupful of flour, one-half teaspoonful of salt, two of baking powder, and if necessary thin with cold milk; bake slowly.

CORN MEAL CAKES.

One cupful of milk, one of water, one-half cupful of yeast, salt, corn meal and flour (use twice as much corn meal as you do of flour), make a sponge about as stiff as bread sponge, let it rise over night; in the morning, add two well beaten eggs and a little soda; bake on a hot griddle.   MRS. F. M. BUZZELL.

FLANNEL CAKES.

Heat a pint of sweet milk, add two heaping teaspoonfuls of butter, let it melt, then add a pint of cold milk, the well-beaten yolks of four eggs, a little salt, four tablespoonfuls of potato yeast, and sufficient flour to make a stiff batter; set in a warm place to rise; let it stand three or four hours or over night; add the whites beaten to a stiff froth just before you bake.

GRAHAM GRIDDLE CAKES.

One pint of milk scalded and cooled, one cupful of whole wheat flour, one cupful of white flour, one-fourth cupful of liquid yeast; let it rise over night; in the morning, add half a teaspoonful of salt, one table-spoonful of molasses, one saltspoonful of soda; if too thick, add a little warm water.

POTATO PANCAKES.

Grate twelve good-sized potatoes and let them stand a few minutes, dip off the water which rises to the top and add the yolks of four eggs well beaten, one tablespoonful of flour and a little salt; lastly, the whites of the eggs beaten to a stiff froth. As the mixture is quite stiff, it will be necessary to flatten the cakes on the griddle. More grease must be used in frying them than for ordinary griddle cakes.

Mrs. T. J. Cunningham.

WHEAT BATTER CAKES.

One quart of sour milk, one of wheat flour, three eggs beaten separately, a tablespoonful of melted butter, two level teaspoonfuls of soda. Put the soda in the flour, mix it in well, and then add the flour to the milk; add the whites of the eggs just before baking on griddle.

Mrs. Geo. C. Ginty.

FRITTERS.

FRITTER BATTER FOR OYSTERS, CLAMS AND TRIPE.

One-half a cupful of milk or water, yolks of two well-beaten eggs, one tablespoonful of olive oil, a good pinch of salt, one cupful of flour, one tablespoonful of lemon juice; and lastly, the white of the eggs beaten to a stiff froth. This batter will keep several days.

APPLE FRITTERS.

Core and pare apples but do not break them; cut them in slices about a third of an inch in thickness, leaving the opening in the center; sprinkle with sugar, lemon and spice, dip in fritter batter and fry in hot lard, drain as you take from the fat and sprinkle with soft sugar. For your batter, use the yokes of two well-beaten

eggs, a teaspoonful of sugar, one-half a cupful of milk, a little salt and one cupful of flour; add the whites of the eggs the last thing and have them beaten to a stiff froth.   Mrs. R. F. Wilson,
Eau Claire, Wis.

CORN FRITTERS.

One can of corn, one and one-half cupfuls of milk, one egg, one tablespoonful of sugar, one heaping cupful of flour, one heaping teaspoonful of baking powder; salt and pepper; fry in a frying-pan with butter. One tablespoonful of the batter makes a good-sized fritter.

Miss Ida Z. Palmer.

QUEEN FRITTERS.

One · pint of water, four ounces of butter, eight ounces of flour; put water in sauce pan, and when it boils, put the flour in all at one time, and stir and beat till it is a smooth and well-cooked mass. Take off and let cool for ten minutes. Add, one at a time, ten eggs, which beat into the mixture till absorbed (do not beat eggs before adding to the paste) add at the last, a trifle of salt unless the butter is salt. Fry in spoonfuls, dropped into plenty of lard. Half of this quantity is sufficient for an ordinary family. Do not use soda or baking powder.   Mrs. Miller,
Spooner, Wis.

SPANISH FRITTERS.

One-half pint of water, three ounces of butter, two ounces of sugar; boil these together a couple of minutes, throw in five ounces of flour, beat till smooth, let it cool a little, then add four eggs—one at a time—beat them in smoothly; lastly, add a teaspoonful of vanilla; fry slowly in plenty of lard, like doughnuts; add powdered sugar before serving. This is a dessert sufficient for a large family. Mrs. Chas. White.

Green Bay, Wis.

We cultivate literature upon a little oatmeal.

‑‑Sydney Smith.

MUSH.

CORNMEAL MUSH.

One quart of boiling water, one pint of corn meal. one tablespoonful of flour, one pint of cold milk (mush will brown better in frying if you use all milk). put one quart of water on to boil, mix as smoothly as possible the corn meal, flour and salt with the milk; stir this slowly with the boiling water. Eat hot with cream, or cut in slices when perfectly cold, and fry in butter. You can use water instead of milk if you cannot get the milk.

OATMEAL MUSH.

One cupful of oatmeal, a teaspoonful of salt, one even quart of boiling water; put the meal and salt in the top of a double boiler, add the boiling water, take it out of the lower boiler and let it cook rapidly on the stove five or ten minutes, stirring occasionally, set back into the boiler again, and let it cook about an hour; just before you remove it from the fire. stir it up so that the steam may escape, and it also makes it dryer.

WHOLE WHEAT MUSH.

Five cupfuls of boiling water, one cupful of whole wheat flour, a little salt. Boil five hours.

And then to breakfast, with
What appetite you have.
—HENRY VIII.

BREAKFAST AND TEA DISHES.

Croquettes should always be rolled in the *cracker or
bread crumbs first*, then in egg and so on, as often as the
rule requires.

If you *bake rice once* you will never boil it again.
It comes from the *oven*, delicious, appetizing food; from
the water, a sticky, tasteless substance.

Do not chop hash too fine. It makes it soft and
mushy. There is a happy medium about the size of a
small white bean. Hash is much nicer baked in the
oven.

BREAKFAST DISH.
(For a cold morning.)

Take large green "bell peppers," cut off the tops
and remove the seeds. Fill with chopped veal and
crumbs, season and prepare the same as for croquettes;
put a few crumbs on top of each and bake in oven.
They look very pretty and are delicious to the taste.

MRS. WM. O'NEIL.

BAKED HASH.

Remove all surplus fat and bits of gristle from
boiled corned beef, chop fine; to one-third corned beef
add two-thirds of chopped cold, boiled potatoes, and a

small onion if you like; season with pepper and salt, place in an earthen dish, dredge a little flour over it, pour in at the sides water enough to come up nearly level with top of hash; bake one hour in oven; when nearly done, add a piece of butter; stir through the hash.

Mrs. T. M. Cary.

BREAKFAST HASH.

Chop cold, corned beef into cubes; add one-third of cold, boiled potatoes, cut into the same size; put in one raw onion, chopped fine, enough butter to keep perfectly moist; then fry until brown.

"Long Lake Delicacy."

BROWN STEW.

Take any scraps of cold meat, cut into dice, brown with one tablespoonful of butter and two of flour, salt and pepper to the taste, flavor with onions if liked, then stir in water until a thick gravy is formed, and serve hot.   Mrs. H. H. Hurd.

BAKED RICE.

Wash a cupful of rice, put it in a pudding dish that will hold a quart of milk or more, add a little salt and a piece of butter, put in the oven and bake until the milk is all absorbed into the rice (about three quarters of an hour). Do not let it cook dry. You can eat cream and sugar on it, or serve as a vegetable with meats.   Mrs. G. C. Ginty.

CHICKEN CROQUETTES—No. 1.

The meat of a well-boiled chicken, chopped fine and seasoned with pepper and salt, mix with it a quarter as much cracker crumbs, make into balls with two tablespoonfuls melted butter and a little of the broth, roll in cracker crumbs, and then in beaten egg, then in cracker crumbs again; fry in hot lard like fried cakes. Mrs. E. M. Miles.

CHICKEN CROQUETTES—No. 2.

Chop very fine the meat of two chickens, season with pepper, salt and one-half of a saltspoonful of grated nutmeg, a tablespoonful of parsley, melt in a stew-pan six ounces of butter, cook half an onion in it a short time, take out the onion, add two even tablespoonfuls of flour and a pint of the broth the chicken was boiled in, add a gill of sweet cream, let it boil up, add the chicken, stir well, put away in a dish to cool. Form into oval balls, roll in beaten yolks of eggs and cracker dust; fry in hot lard. Do not think it too thin when put away to cool, as cooling hardens them, and they can be easily moulded. They are not nice if too stiff. Veal can be used instead of chicken; about a quart of chopped veal would be equal to the chicken. Mrs. Wm. O'Neill.

CHICKEN CROQUETTES—No. 3.

One large chicken, one-quarter pound of butter, one-quarter pint of sweet cream, three tablespoonfuls of flour; salt, pepper, the juice of a lemon, and one dozen mushrooms chopped fine; cut your chicken like dice; melt the butter, put in flour, add the cream, boil for a few minutes, and if too thick add a little broth to thin it, put in chicken, mushrooms and lemon juice, one-half gill of Madeira wine, and spread on platter to cool;

when cold, cut in small pieces, roll in egg and bread crumbs and fry in hot lard.

Mrs. A. J. McGilvray.

ESCALLOPED CHEESE.

Three eggs beaten separately, one cupful of bread crumbs soaked in two cups of milk; one teacupful of grated cheese: a little salt: bake half an hour.

Mrs. J. C. Mitchell,
Chicago, Ill.

EGG GEMS.

Mix together any kind of cold meats, chopped fine, with an equal quantity of bread crumbs, season with salt, pepper, butter and a little milk, fill some buttered gem pans with the mixture, then carefully break an egg on the top of each, sprinkle cracker crumbs, salt and pepper over the top, bake eight minutes. A little grated cheese may be added to the cracker, if desired.

Mrs. T. W. Martin.

EGG ROLLS.

Six eggs, well beaten, one pint of milk, salt, five even tablespoonfuls of flour, grease the griddle, pour over thin, brown on one side, cut in lengths, and roll each piece up on the griddle.

Mrs. S. J. Yundt.

EGG VERMICELLI.

Toast four slices of bread, boil three eggs twenty minutes, one pint of boiling milk, one-half teaspoonful of salt, one-fourth teaspoonful of pepper, two table-spoonfuls of butter, two heaping tablespoonfuls of flour, mix all together and cook, put whites of eggs through a fruit press, mix with the other ingredients and pour over the toast, put yolks through the press and garnish the top.

EGGS (Baked).

Beat the whites of six eggs until stiff and dry, form them into a mound on a platter, make six little nests in the mound, drop the yolks into them without breaking. Put salt, pepper and butter on each. Then brown over in a very hot oven. COOKING SCHOOL.

EGGS (Deviled)—No. 1.

Boil hard six eggs, remove the shells and halve each egg, slipping the yolks into a bowl. Prepare a dressing for them as follows: Two tablespoonfuls of melted butter, two of vinegar, one of sugar, one small teaspoonful of French mustard, salt and pepper, add the yolks, rub all together until free from lumps, make into balls and replace in the whites, cut off the end of the egg so that it will stand upon the platter; garnish with parsley. MRS. H. DARLAND,

Newark, N. Y.

EGGS (Deviled)—No. 2.

Boil twelve eggs fifteen minutes, cut lengthwise, take out yolks and mash them, add to them one tablespoonful of olive oil or butter, one teaspoonful of French mustard, two heaping tablespoonfuls of finely chopped ham; salt and pepper to taste. Rub all together. Fill the whites with this mixture, and serve for tea or lunch.

EGGS (Boiled "to the Queen's Taste").

Have the water boiling, put in the eggs and set the kettle on the back of the stove for five minutes.

Dr. Charles A. Hayes.

FRENCH TOAST.

Put one quart of milk in a double boiler, add two eggs well beaten, a little salt and a small piece of butter, dip slices of bread in the milk and fry in butter on a hot griddle until brown, place on a platter; boil milk until it thickens, and pour over the toast; if it does not thicken enough, add a little flour.

Mrs. V. W. Bayless,
Minneapolis, Minn.

FRIED CREAM.

One-half pound flour, six eggs, mix well together, dilute in one quart of milk, salt, flavor with lemon or vanilla, put on fire and stir fifteen minutes, add four ounces of sugar, yolks of four eggs; spread on platter to get cold; cut in squares, roll in egg and bread crumbs, fry in hot lard. Mrs. A. J. McGilvray.

GREEN CORN BREAKFAST CAKES.

Take one dozen ears of corn, quite well matured, grate, add two tablespoonfuls of flour, one cupful of milk, and three eggs, the whole to be mixed together and beaten to a batter; salt to taste; bake like griddle cakes. They should be sent to the table as fast as baked. This is delicious, and if once tried, will become a favorite. Mrs. H. H. Todd.

HARRISON CREAM TOAST.

Melt in one pint of morning's milk one large table-spoonful of butter, one teaspoonful of flour, stir it smooth in a little of the milk, two eggs beaten separately; heat, but not boil milk and eggs, or it will curdle and loose the appearance of cream; add salt; when hot, dip the toast and pour the remainder over it; serve hot. Mrs. H. H. Todd.

HOMINY CROQUETTES.

Warm a pint of cooked hominy in one or two table-spoonfuls of hot milk; add the beaten yolk of one egg, and salt to taste, cool, shape, roll in beaten egg and crumbs, and fry. Mrs. Judson.

MACARONI—No. 1.

Five tablespoonfuls of grated cheese, one of flour, one of butter, one egg, one-half a cupful of cream; salt and pepper; put over the fire and stir until the cheese is dissolved. Boil some macaroni in salted water about fifteen minutes, drain off the water, put milk over it and boil again for a few minutes; stir all together and bake half an hour.

Mrs. A. J. McGilvray.

MACARONI—No. 2.

Boil macaroni in milk and water until soft and well swollen out. Put a layer in a shallow baking dish, salt and pepper it, cut small slices of cheese over it, with small pieces of butter; repeat this until the dish is full. Put milk and water in until it comes up so

that you can see it on the sides of the dish, beat an egg
and pour over the top and bake until it is dry enough
to look and taste well.   Mrs. G. C. Ginty.

MACARONI—No. 3.

Break one-half a pound of macaroni into inch
lengths, boil in water slightly salted until tender,
drain, put nearly one-half a cupful of cream into a
saucepan, scald, and salt to taste, add one-half a tablespoonful of butter, then the macaroni, and heat. Put
two tablespoonfuls of cream into a small saucepan, heat,
stir in a tablespoonful of butter, a little pepper, tablespoonful of flour wet with cold milk, four tablespoonfuls of grated cheese; when this is dissolved, add one
beaten egg. Pour the macaroni into a baking dish and
cover with the cheese mixture. Strew the top with
fine bread crumbs and brown quickly.

Mrs. Emma Miller,

Beatrice, Neb.

MACARONI CROQUETTES.

One pint cold boiled macaroni chopped fine, heat
and moisten with a little white sauce (found in " Catchups
and Sauces" in this book), add the beaten yolk of one
egg, two table spoonfuls of grated cheese, salt and
pepper to taste; cool, make into balls, roll in crumbs,
then in egg, then in crumbs again; fry in hot lard.

Mrs. S. J. Yundt.

OMELET (Plain).

Nine eggs, three tablespoonfuls of butter, one-half
cupful of flour, one small cupful of milk, salt and
pepper to taste, beat the yolks light, mix baking

powder size of a pea in the flour; beat the whites very stiff and pour the mixture over them, not mixing them together but dipping from top to bottom; put a spoonful in a hot buttered pan, and as it browns roll over and over. Serve immediately.

Mrs. J. W. Squires.

OMELET (Delicate).

The yolks of six eggs and whites of three, one tablespoonful of flour, dissolved in a cup of sweet milk, a little salt, beat the yolks well and mix with the milk, melt a tablespoonful of butter in a pan, pour in the mixture and bake in a hot oven; when it puffs up, pour over it the remaining three whites well beaten: return it to the oven and let it bake a delicate brown. Serve hot. Mrs. E. Patton.

OMELET (French).

One cupful of boiling milk, one tablespoonful of butter, put this on one cupful of bread crumbs (crumbs must be light), add salt, pepper and the yolks of six eggs, well beaten, mix thoroughly, and, lastly, add the six whites, beaten to a stiff froth. Have your pan hot, and grease well with butter. Bake ten minutes.

Mrs. C. P. Barker.

OMELET (Shamrock).

Take seven eggs, one small teacupful of milk, mix one teaspoonful of flour, one-half teaspoonful of salt; beat the yolks, salt and flour together; then add the milk; beat the whites to a stiff froth; have ready a hot pan; put in a lump of butter size of an acorn; add the whites to the yolks; pour into the pan; watch carefully. When done, fold over and serve in a hot dish.

Mrs. Kyle.

POTATO ROLLS.

One dozen good-sized potatoes, boiled and mashed, add the yolks of two well-beaten eggs, one large tablespoonful of cream, two tablespoonfuls of butter, one-half tablespoonful of salt, spoonful of nutmeg; beat thoroughly; let the mixture cool; make in rolls flattened at each end; dip in egg, then in cracker dust; fry brown in hot lard. Mrs. Wm. O'Neil.

RICE CROQUETTES.

Boil, without stirring, a cup of rice until tender; while warm, add two well-beaten eggs and a small piece of butter; make into rolls and dip into either cracker crumbs or flour, and fry in lard. Miss Wilson,

Menomonee, Wis.

SUNDAY MORNING DISH.

Make a kettle of corn-meal mush on Saturday. Sunday morning cut in nice square slices, roll in egg, then in cracker crumbs, fry rich brown.

Mrs. McCluer,

Stillwater, Minn.

SHEPHERD'S PIE.

Cold meat, chopped up and seasoned properly, put into a pudding dish; moisten the meat with hot water; put a layer of mashed potatoes over meat about two inches thick: put a little butter on potatoes and bake.

Mrs. Kyle.

TEA DISH.

Melt two tablespoonfuls of butter in a frying pan, add one teaspoonful of flour and stir until smooth, then add one cupful of water, or stock if you have it, season with salt and pepper; when it boils, add one quart of coarsely chopped cold veal; let this heat thoroughly, then serve it on slices of nicely browned toast. A poached egg may be put on the center of each slice if wished. Mrs. Wm. O'Neil.

VEAL CROQUETTES.

Chop cold veal fine, season highly with salt, pepper, a little cayenne, onion juice, celery salt and parsley. Moisten with beaten egg and white sauce (found in "Catchups and Sauces" in this book), shape in rolls, roll in fine bread crumbs, then in egg, in crumbs again, and fry in hot lard. Cooking School.

VEAL SUPPER DISH.

Take a shank of veal and boil it until the flesh drops off, chop into inch squares, boil the water the veal cooks in to a jelly and cool it; boil six eggs hard; slice them and line a dish; put the meat into the dish and pour the jelly over and set on ice. When you serve, turn the form out on a platter and garnish with celery leaves. Season it to taste when you take it from the pot. "Aunty Kyle."

WELSH RAREBIT.

Grate one-quarter pound of rich cheese, moisten with one-half cupful of warm water, and same quantity of milk, add one well-beaten egg, piece of butter the size of an egg, put in a pan and boil three minutes, then add a teaspoonful of mustard and a dash of cayenne pepper. Have ready some buttered toast moistened with hot water. Pour the cheese over it and serve while hot.

CAKES AND FROSTINGS.

In making fruit cake, do not chop citron but cut crosswise of the melon-shaped pieces, in long, thin slices; put a layer of the dough (containing all the other fruit) in your pan and lay around pieces of the citron about an inch from the sides of the pan, and so on until you have used the required quantity. This prevents it from burning on the bottom and sides of the pan, makes it smooth for the icing, and, when you cut your cake, cuts the citron just right. If you have a large fruit cake to bake, make a dough of graham flour and water, put this half an inch thick in the bottom of your pan, put a greased paper over it and then put in the cake dough; this prevents burning on the bottom, for a large cake has to be in the oven so long it is almost impossible to keep it from burning.

Bake cookies on the dripper turned "up side down," and they will not burn.

ALMOND CREAM CAKE.

Two cupfuls of pulverized sugar, one-quarter cupful of butter, one cupful of sweet milk, three cupfuls of flour, two and one-half teaspoonfuls of baking powder, whites of four eggs beaten very light, one-half teaspoonful of vanilla, bake in four layers, whip one cupful of sweet cream to a froth, stirring gradually into it half a cupful of pulverized sugar, a few drops of vanilla, one pound of almonds, blanched and chopped fine; spread thickly between layers; frost top and sides.

Mrs. J. Rumsey.

ALMOND CUSTARD CAKE—No. 1.

Three cupfuls of sugar, one cupful of butter, one cupful of sour milk (loppered), one teaspoonful of soda, five eggs, four cupfuls of flour; bake in layers, and put together with the custard used in "Almond Custard Cake—No. 2."

ALMOND CUSTARD CAKE—No. 2.

One-half cupful of butter, two cupfuls of sugar, one-half cupful of sweet milk, two and one-half cupfuls of flour, five eggs, two teaspoonfuls of baking powder.

Custard.—Two eggs, one tablespoonful of corn starch, one pint of milk, make very sweet, one pound of almonds, blanched and chopped fine; cook the custard until thick, add the almonds, and spread between layers.   Mrs. H. J. Goddard.

ANGELS' FOOD.

Use the whites of eleven eggs, one and one-half tumblerfuls of sifted granulated sugar, one tumblerful of sifted flour, one teaspoonful of vanilla, one teaspoonful of cream of tartar, sift the flour four times, add the cream of tartar and sift again, measure it before adding the cream of tartar, sift the sugar and measure it, beat the eggs to a stiff froth on a large platter; on the same platter, add the sugar lightly, then the flour very gently, then the vanilla; do not stop beating until you put it in the pan to bake; bake forty minutes in a moderate oven; try with a straw; do not open the oven until the cake has been in fifteen minutes; turn the pan upside down to cool. When cold, use a knife to loosen around the sides if it does not drop out before. Never grease the pan; the tumbler for measuring must hold two and one-fourth gills; the pan should have feet at the top to prevent the cake touching when turned to cool.   Mrs. Hiram Allen,

Bradford, Pa.

"AUNTY BEALL'S" SPONGE CAKE.

Eight eggs, whites and yolks beaten separately, two tumblerfuls of sugar, two tumblerfuls of flour, flavor with lemon; bake in a sheet. Beat the whites to a stiff froth, add the yolks to the whites which have been previously beaten very light, stir in slowly the sugar, and lastly the flour; put together as quickly as possible; do not beat; bake in a moderate oven. Make this cake on a large platter.

BANANA CAKE.

Two teacupfuls of sugar, scant half-cupful of butter, four eggs, three cupfuls of flour, one cupful of sweet milk, two teaspoonfuls of baking powder, cream, butter and sugar together, and beat whites of eggs to a stiff froth, bake in layers, then make a plain frosting and spread between layers. Slice bananas thin and spread them over the frosting so that each slice will touch the other; finish the cake with a plain frosting.

Mrs. A. J. Bate.

BLACK CAKE.

Three cupfuls of sugar, one and one-half cupfuls of butter, one cupful of molasses, five eggs, one tablespoonful of cloves, two tablespoonfuls of cinnamon, two of nutmeg, a wine glass of wine or brandy, one teaspoonful of soda, one pound of flour, two pounds of fruit.

Mrs. James Comerford.

BLITZKUCHEN, OR LIGHTNING CAKE.

Nine ounces of butter, nine ounces of sugar, nine ounces of flour, four whole eggs, clear the butter (that is, just melt it, then pour off top so that no salt remains in it); then add sugar, eggs and flour; spread in large bread pans very thin. Put chopped almonds, sugar and cinnamon on top, and bake till a very light brown, then cut in diamonds.   Mrs. Himmelsbach.

BREAD CAKE—No. 1.

One-half pound of almonds, chopped fine, yolks of twelve eggs, three-fourths pound of pulverized sugar, grated rind of one lemon, one teaspoonful of cloves, one teaspoonful of cinnamon, one-fourth pound of pulverized dry bread, one teaspoonful of baking powder, add whites of twelve eggs, beaten to stiff froth, and almonds when ready to put in oven; bake very slowly.

Mrs. Himmelsbach.

BREAD CAKE—No. 2.

One teacupful of bread sponge, two-thirds cupful of butter, one and one-half cupfuls of sugar, two eggs, one teaspoonful of soda, one teaspoonful of cinnamon, one-half teaspoonful of cloves, two cupfuls of flour, one cupful of stoned raisins; let it rise half an hour, and bake in a slow oven.   Mrs. II. H. Todd.

BRIDE'S CAKE.

Whites of sixteen eggs, four cupfuls of pulverized sugar, one scant cupful of butter, one cupful of sweet milk, five cupfuls of flour, three teaspoonfuls of baking powder, flavor with lemon or almond; just before baking, add a tablespoonful of brandy, cream the butter and sugar, add the milk, then half the flour, then a portion of the whites of the eggs, beaten to a high froth, then more flour and the rest of the eggs; get together as quickly as possible and do not beat the mixture.   Bake in a moderate oven.

Mrs. R. F. Wilson,
Eau Claire, Wis.

BURNETT CAKE.

One and one-half cupfuls of sugar, one-half cupful of butter, one cupful of sweet milk, whites of four eggs and yolks of three, three cupfuls of flour, three teaspoonfuls of baking powder; bake in dripping pan, sift one-half cupful of sugar over top before baking; flavor with lemon.   Mrs. T. W. Martin.

CARAMEL CAKE—No. 1.

One cupful of sugar, one-half cupful of butter, one-half cupful of sweet milk, whites of four eggs, two cupfuls of flour, two teaspoonfuls of baking powder.

Caramel for the Top.—Six heaping tablespoonfuls of

grated chocolate, two eggs, one cupful of brown sugar, one teaspoonful of vanilla, scant one-half cup of sweet milk; mix together and stir while boiling until thick.

MISS FANNY GINTY.

CARAMEL CAKE—No. 2.

One cupful of sugar, one and one-half cupfuls of flour, two eggs, one-half cupful of sweet milk, butter size of an egg, two teaspoonfuls of baking powder.

Frosting.—Take one cupful of brown sugar, one-half cake sweet chocolate, one-half cupful sweet milk, butter size of an egg, two teaspoonfuls of vanilla, mix thoroughly and cook as syrup; let it cool and spread on cake as soon as taken from the oven.

MRS. J. COMERFORD.

CHOCOLATE CAKE—No. 1.

Whites of four eggs, one cupful of sugar, one-half cupful of butter, one and one-half cupfuls of flour, one-half cupful of sweet milk, one and one-half teaspoonfuls of baking powder; beat the butter and sugar until light, add the milk, then the flour and beaten whites; when well beaten, divide in equal parts, into one-half grate one-half cake sweet chocolate; bake in layers; put together with boiled frosting or custard; alternate white and dark layers.

Custard.—Add one-half tablespoonful of butter to one cupful of milk, let it come to a boil, stir one egg beaten with one-half cupful of sugar and one teaspoonful of corn starch into the milk; flavor with vanilla or lemon.

MRS. T. M. CARY.

CHOCOLATE CAKE—No. 2.

One cupful of sugar, one-half cupful of butter, one-half cupful of milk, two cupfuls of flour, two eggs, two teaspoonfuls of baking powder; bake in thin layers.

For the Jelly.—Grate one-half cake of sweet chocolate, one-half cupful of sweet milk, yolk of one egg, one teaspoonful of vanilla, one cupful of sugar, boil until stiff like jelly; when cold, spread between the layers; the jelly should be made first.   Mrs. Himmelsbach.

CHOCOLATE CAKE—No. 3.

The whites of three eggs, beaten to a stiff froth, one teacupful of sugar, one-half cupful of sweet milk, one-fourth cupful of butter, one heaping teaspoonful of baking powder, one coffeecupful of flour; flavor with one-half teaspoonful of lemon and vanilla each;. bake in square tins.

Frosting.—Take a small cupful of granulated sugar and wet it with five teaspoonfuls of water; let it boil; while boiling, put in one teaspoonful of vinegar; boil until clear and ropy, then pour it over the white of one egg, beaten to a stiff froth, and then stir in one-fourth cake of Baker's Chocolate, grated; beat until nearly cold, and spread over the cake; then make a white frosting, same as above, leaving out the chocolate; flavor with a few drops each of lemon and vanilla, and spread on the chocolate frosting.   Mrs. B. E. Ried.

CIRCLE CAKE.

One egg, one cupful of sugar, two cupfuls of flour, one-third cupful of butter, one-half cupful of sweet milk, one teaspoonful of cream of tartar, one-half teaspoonful of soda, or two even teaspoonfuls of baking powder; flavor with rose or lemon.   MRS. R. B. CLARK,

COCOANUT BAR.

Bake a white cake in a dripper; when cold, cut in squares a pretty size for the cake basket, have ready a good supply of frosting made with pulverized sugar (boiled will not do, as it hardens before you can use it); pour a box of grated cocoanut into a shallow dish, take a square of the cake on a fork, and with a spoon, cover it on all sides with the frosting; then roll in the cocoanut until it is covered.   Put near the fire to dry; when dry fill your cake basket with the bars.   After you have made two or three you will have no trouble; this is a fussy cake to make, but is so delicious and looks so pretty after it is made, you can afford to make it on grand occasions.   MRS. LESLIE WILLSON,

Eau Claire, Wis.

COCOANUT CAKE.

Two cupfuls of sugar, one cupful of butter, one-half cupful of sweet milk, three cupfuls of sifted flour, three teaspoonfuls of baking powder, five eggs.

Frosting for Layers and Top.—Whites of three eggs, one cupful of pulverized sugar, one cupful of cocoanut.

MRS. H. J. GODDARD.

COCOANUT JUMBLES.

Two cupfuls of sugar, one cupful of butter, two eggs, three cupfuls of flour, small teaspoonful of soda, one grated cocoanut or one cupful of prepared cocoanut.

MISS ETTA CARY,

Binghampton, N. Y.

COCOANUT MACAROONS.

Beat the whites of two eggs to a stiff froth, add one-half pound of sugar, one-half pound of grated cocoanut, beat until stiff enough to form in little balls the size of a nutmeg, dip the finger in cold water, and smooth them into any form you like; bake slowly on a greased paper for three-quarters of an hour.

COCOANUT COOKIES.

One and one-half cupfuls of sugar, three-fourths cupful of butter, one-half cupful of sweet milk, two eggs, one cupful of grated cocoanut, one-half teaspoonful of soda, one teaspoonful of vanilla, flour enough to make as soft as possible, and roll out; bake in a hot oven.

Mrs. L. H. Cushing.

COCOANUT POUND CAKE.

Two cupfuls of pulverized sugar, two-thirds cupful of butter, one cupful of sweet milk, one-half cupful of corn starch, two and one-half cupfuls of flour, whites of five eggs, one and one-half teaspoonfuls of baking powder, one cupful of cocoanut; flavor.

Mrs. H. L. Cruttenden,
Northfield, Minn.

COFFEE CAKE—No. 1.

Four cupfuls of flour, one cupful of butter, one cupful of coffee prepared as for table, one cupful of molasses, one cupful of brown sugar, one pound raisins, two eggs, one teaspoonful of soda, one teaspoonful of spices of all kinds.

Mrs. A. S. Stiles.

COFFEE CAKE—No. 2.

Two cupfuls of brown sugar, two small cupfuls of

butter, one cupful of molasses, one cupful of strong coffee (cold), five cupfuls flour, one pound of raisins, one pound of currents, one-quarter pound of citron, one teaspoonful of soda, one tablespoonful of cloves, one tablespoonful of cinnamon, one tablespoonful of ground coffee, one nutmeg, one wine glassful of wine, four eggs.

COOKIES.

Two cupfuls of sugar, one cupful of butter, one-half cupful of sour milk, two eggs, one-half teaspoonful of soda ; flavor with lemon ; sift sugar over the top before baking.   Mrs. H. H. Todd.

CREAM CAKE.

One cupful of sugar, one-half cupful of butter, one-half cupful of sweet milk, one-half cupful of corn starch, one and one-half cupfuls of flour, one teaspoonful of baking powder, whites of four eggs.

Cream.—Whip one cupful of sweet cream, add sugar and flavoring to taste, and spread between layers, or make a boiled frosting, and first spread between each layer, then the cream. It will keep better with the frosting, but is better without if eaten fresh.

Mrs. F. T. Condit.

CREAM COOKIES.

Two cupfuls of sugar, one cupful of butter, one cupful of sour cream, two eggs well beaten, one teaspoonful of soda, stir the butter and sugar to a cream, a little salt : flavor to taste.   Mrs. J. Rumsey.

CREAM GINGER CAKE.

One cupful of sour cream, one cupful of molasses, one egg, a little salt, one teaspoonful of ginger, one teaspoonful of soda, cinnamon if you like; no rule for flour; make as soft as can be and not fall.

Mrs. H. H. Todd.

CREAM PUFFS.

Boil in half a pint of water three-quarters cupful of butter, stir in one and three-quarters cupfuls of flour, take from the fire and put into a large bowl and stir in five eggs, one at a time, without beating, add one-half teaspoonful of soda.   Drop in small bits about a tablespoonful on a greased paper in a dripping pan; bake in a quick oven.

Filling.—One quart of milk, five eggs, one and one-half cupfuls of sugar, two tablespoonfuls of corn starch, flavor with vanilla. When cakes are cool cut open and fill.   Miss Angie Wilson,

Menomonie, Wis.

CRULLERS—No. 1.

Dissolve a teaspoonful of soda in four tablespoonfuls of milk, four tablespoonfuls of melted butter, one teaspoonful of salt, beat four eggs with six heaping tablespoonfuls of sugar, add half a nutmeg. These will keep for weeks if put in a jar and covered. Omitting the salt will keep them from being brittle.

Miss J. E. Dickinson.

CRULLERS—No. 2.

Five tablespoonfuls of sugar, five tablespoonfuls of sweet cream, three teaspoonfuls of alcohol, two teaspoonfuls baking powder, add flour, roll out thin as pie crust, and fry as doughnuts.   Mrs. Piper,

Eau Claire, Wis.

CUSTARD CAKE No. 1.

One cupful of sugar, one-half cupful of butter (scant), whites of four eggs, one-half cupful of sweet milk, one heaping teaspoonful of baking powder, one and one-half cupfuls of flour.

Custard for Cake.—One and one-half cupfuls of milk, yolks of four eggs, one tablespoonful of corn starch, one-half cupful of sugar, a pinch of salt; cook until thick; flavor with lemon, vanilla or chocolate.

MRS. W. IRVINE.

CUSTARD CAKE No. 2.

One cupful of sugar, one and one-third cupfuls of flour, three eggs, one heaping teaspoonful of baking powder, one tablespoonful of water, bake in round tins, cut in two and spread between and on the top a custard made as follows: One pint of sweet milk, one cupful of white sugar, two tablespoonfuls of corn starch, two eggs; beat thoroughly the sugar, eggs and corn starch; stir into the boiling milk; add butter the size of an egg, three teaspoonfuls of vanilla; cook until thick. The white of one egg can be saved to frost the top.

MRS. A. HOFFMAN.

DARK CHOCOLATE CAKE—No. 1.

Cream one-half cupful of butter, gradually add one and one-half cupfuls of sugar, grate one-quarter of a cake of Baker's Chocolate, add five more tablespoonfuls of sugar and three tablespoonfuls of boiling water, put on the stove and stir until smooth and glossy, then add it to the beaten butter and sugar; add the beaten yolks of three eggs, one-half cupful of milk, one and three-quarters cupfuls of flour, in which one teaspoonful of cream of tartar and one-half teaspoonful of soda have been thoroughly mixed; add the whites of three eggs, beaten to a stiff froth, bake twenty minutes in a moderate oven. Put together with "Chocolate Frosting No. 2." English walnuts, chopped fine and sprinkled on the frosting between the layers, is very nice.

Mrs. J. W. Squires.

DARK CHOCOLATE CAKE—No. 2.

One cupful of sugar, one tablespoonful of butter, one cupful of milk, two cupfuls of flour, two eggs beaten separately, two heaping teaspoonfuls of baking powder, one-quarter cake Baker's Chocolate grated in a small half cupful of milk (this in addition to the cupful of milk), boil in a basin, set in hot water until like a paste, then add one cupful of sugar, yolk of one egg, two teaspoonfuls of vanilla; let it cool slightly and stir into the cake; bake in four layers and put together with any chocolate frosting. Mrs. Whitney,

Green Bay.

DARK CHOCOLATE CAKE—No. 3.

Two cupfuls of sugar, one-half cupful of butter, one-half cupful of thick sour milk, three eggs, one-half teaspoonful of soda, one-fourth of a cake of Baker's chocolate dissolved in one-half cupful of hot water, one and one-half teaspoonfuls of vanilla, a little salt, two cupfuls of flour; bake in a loaf forty minutes.

Mrs. Wm. O'Neil.

DELICATE CAKE—No. 1.

Two cupfuls of sugar, one-half cupful of butter, whites of six eggs beaten to a stiff froth, three-fourths cupful of sweet milk, three cupfuls of flour, two teaspoonfuls of baking powder or one teaspoonful of cream of tartar, one-half teaspoonful of soda; flavor with lemon or almond.   Mrs. A. J. Cady.

DELICATE CAKE—No. 2.

One cupful of butter, three cupfuls of sugar, whites of ten eggs, four and one-half cupfuls of flour, one cupful sweet cream, three teaspoonfuls of baking powder; flavor.   Mrs. Peter Leonard,

Fifield, Wis.

DOUGHNUTS.

One-half cupful of yeast, or a good yeast cake, one cupful of lard, three cupfuls of sweet milk, two cupfuls of sugar, if you want them quite sweet a little more sugar, four eggs, one teaspoonful of soda, nutmeg and cinnamon; warm milk, lard and sugar together, make sponge in the afternoon, put eggs and soda in when you knead it up at night; cut them out in the morning and let them rise again on a board near the fire. Keep warm all the time.   Mrs. S. F. Cary,

Binghamton, N. Y.

DOLLY VARDEN CAKE.

Two cupfuls of sugar, two-thirds cupful of butter, one cupful of sweet milk, three cupfuls of flour, three eggs, two teaspoonfuls of baking powder, flavor with lemon, bake half in jelly tins; to the remainder add one tablespoonful of molasses, one teacupful of chopped raisins, one-half cupful of citron, one teaspoonful each of cinnamon and cloves. Bake same as white cake and put together with frosting, alternating dark and light.

Mrs. D. G. Purman,

Washington, D. C.

ENGLISH NUT CAKE WITH RAISINS.

Two cupfuls of brown sugar, one-half cupful of butter, one scant cupful of sour milk, yolks of five eggs, two cupfuls of flour, one teaspoonful of soda, two teaspoonfuls of cinnamon, one teaspoonful of cloves, one-half nutmeg, one pound of stoned raisins, one pound of English walnuts, one teaspoonful of brandy; save twenty-four halves for top, chop the rest and put in cake. Mrs. T. J. Cunningham.

FIG CAKE—No. 1.

One cupful of sugar, one-half cupful of butter, one-half cupful of sweet milk, one-half cupful of corn starch, one and one-half cupfuls of flour, one teaspoonful of baking powder, whites of four eggs.

Filling.—One pound of figs cut in pieces, two-thirds cupful of sugar, water enough to stew.

Mrs. F. T. Condit.

FIG CAKE—No. 2.

Two teacupfuls of sugar rolled fine, one scant, half teacupful of butter, cream the sugar and butter together, four eggs beaten separately, one cupful of sweet milk, two teaspoonfuls of baking powder, three cupfuls of flour sifted.

Filling.—One pound of figs, one-half cupful of

sugar, one cupful of water, white of one egg, one teaspoonful of vanilla. Let the sugar and water boil until clear, then drop in the figs and boil until tender enough to mash; remove from the fire and cool a little after mashing; stir in the egg slightly beaten, then the vanilla, and spread between layers and frost.

Mrs. A. J. Bate.

FIG CAKE—No. 3.

Beat the yolks of three eggs with not quite two cupfuls of sugar, then add four tablespoonfuls of melted butter, two-thirds cupful of sweet milk, whites of three eggs beaten to a stiff froth, and lastly two cupfuls of flour, and two teaspoonfuls of baking powder. This quantity will make two cakes.

Fig paste for cake.—One pound of raisins, one pound of almonds, three-quarters pound of figs, one-half pound of citron; blanch the almonds by pouring hot water over them; chop fine and moisten with brandy or wine; it will require a good-sized cupful; place between layers, first frosting, then fig paste alternately.

Mrs. Daisy Grossman.

FRIED CAKES—No. 1.

One cupful of sugar, two eggs, one cupful of sour milk, two teaspoonfuls of soda, two and one-half tablespoonfuls of butter, salt and nutmeg; mix soft as possible.   Mrs. Himmelsbach.

FRIED CAKES—No. 2.

Three eggs, three tablespoonfuls of butter, one cupful of sugar, one cupful of sweet milk, two teaspoonfuls of baking powder, cinnamon or nutmeg to flavor, mix just stiff enough to roll out nicely.

Mrs. Culver,
Bay City, Mich.

FRIED CAKES—No. 3.

Two eggs, one cupful of sour cream, one cupful of sour milk, one cupful of sugar, a little salt, one teaspoonful of soda, a little cream tartar if the milk is not very sour, cinnamon or nutmeg to flavor.

Mrs. J. Comerford.

FRIED CAKES—No. 4.

One cupful of sugar, one cupful of sweet milk, six tablespoonfuls of melted butter, three teaspoonfuls of baking powder. Mix soft; let the sugar and milk stand together twenty minutes; flavor with nutmeg.

Mrs. W. L. Pierce.

FRENCH CAKE.

Cream two cupfuls of sugar and half a cupful of butter, add one cupful of sweet milk, three eggs, yolks and whites beaten separately, sift two tablespoonfuls of baking powder in three cupfuls of flour; flavor to suit; use as a plain or layer cake.

Mrs. Emma Miller,
Nebraska.

FRUIT CAKE FOR A WEDDING.

One and one-half pounds of butter, one and three-quarter pounds of sugar, half brown and half white, two pounds of eggs, well beaten, four pounds of raisins, seeded and chopped, five pounds of English currants.

two pounds of citron, cut fine, two pounds of sifted flour, two nutmegs, as much mace in bulk, one gill to one-half pint of alcohol, into which drop fifteen drops of oil of lemon; weigh your butter, cut it in pieces and put where it will soften (not melt), stir the butter to a cream, add the sugar and stir until white, beat the yolks of the eggs and add to the butter and sugar. Meanwhile, another person should beat the whites to a stiff froth and put them in, then add the spices and flour, and last of all the fruit (except citron); put the citron in three layers, one near the bottom, one about the middle, and the last layer near the top of the cake. As you lay it in, dip a spoon in cold water and smooth over the cake to make it even for the citron. This will make two very large or four good-sized cakes. Bake from three to four hours slowly. It is better to have the baker bake them for you in a brick oven. The cake will keep years.

Mrs. E. D. Stanley.

FRUIT CAKE—No. 1.

Twelve eggs, one pound of butter, one pound of brown sugar, one pound of sifted flour, one-half cupful of black molasses, three pounds of stoned raisins, three pounds of currants, one pound of citron, one-half cupful of brandy, one and one-half pounds of almonds, one tablespoonful of cloves, two of cinnamon and allspice, one-half teaspoonful of soda, grated rind and juice of one lemon, one nutmeg; beat yolks, butter and sugar together, whites to a stiff froth, and add alternately with flour, then spices and fruit; put in a pan a layer of dough; add citron as in receipt for "Wedding Cake"; bake slowly and evenly four hours or longer.

Mrs. P. Leonard,

Fifield, Wis.

FRUIT CAKE—No. 2.

One cupful of sugar, one cupful of molasses, two cupfuls of flour, one-half cupful of butter, one-half cupful of sour cream, three eggs, one-half teaspoonful of soda, three pounds of stoned raisins, one pound of citron, one pound of figs, one pound of currants, one-half pound of almonds (shelled), one gill of wine, one gill of brandy, one orange, two teaspoonfuls of cinnamon, one teaspoonful of cloves, one teaspoonful of mace, two nutmegs, a little salt.

Mrs. H. L. Cruttenden,

Northfield, Minn.

FRUIT CAKE—No. 3.

One cupful of butter, two cupfuls of sugar, one cupful of sour milk, one cupful of New Orleans molasses, three cupfuls of flour, one teaspoonful of soda, one teaspoonful of cloves, two teaspoonfuls of cinnamon, one pound of raisins, one pound of currants, one-half pound of citron, one-half cupful of nuts, one teaspoonful of vanilla.

Mrs. A. Hoffman.

GINGER COOKIES.

One cupful of butter, one teacupful of sugar, two cupfuls of molasses, one teaspoonful of grated alum, one teaspoonful of ginger, one teaspoonful of cinnamon, four teaspoonfuls of soda, one cupful of boiling water. Take half of the water to dissolve the soda and half for the alum, mix soft and let them stand for two hours, then roll out about one-quarter of an inch thick, adding more flour if needed ; do not cut out with a cake cutter, but in long strips, crease them with a knife in squares and cut apart after baking. These are very nice if made as directed.   MRS. T. M. CARY.

GINGER SNAPS—No. 1.

One cupful of molasses, one-half cupful of butter, one tablespoonful of soda dissolved in one tablespoonful of hot water, one tablespoonful of ginger and cinnamon.   MRS. HERBERT BARKER.

GINGER SNAPS—No. 2.

One cupful of butter, one cupful of brown sugar, one cupful of molasses, two small tablespoonfuls of ginger, one even tablespoonful of soda, one tablespoonful of cinnamon, one egg, stir all together and let it just come to a boil, flour enough to roll very thin, and bake in a hot oven.   MRS. WM. IRVINE.

GINGER SNAPS—No. 3.

One cupful of butter, or part lard, one cupful of molasses, one cupful of sugar, one teaspoonful of cinnamon, one teaspoonful of ginger, two teaspoonfuls of soda, one egg beaten separately, flour enough to roll thin.   MRS. T. M. CARY.

GINGER SNAPS—No. 4.

One cupful of butter, one cupful of sugar, one cupful of molasses, one tablespoonful of ginger, one tablespoonful of cinnamon, two teaspoonfuls of soda, flour enough to roll thin.   MRS. W. L. PIERCE.

GINGER SNAPS—No. 5.

Two cupfuls of molasses, one cupful of brown sugar, one-half cupful of butter, one-half cupful of lard, one heaping tablespoonful of ginger, three tablespoonfuls of water, one good teaspoonful of saleratus, one teaspoonful of cinnamon; boil all together five minutes, then cool and add flour until stiff enough to roll well.

Mrs. Porter,
Baraboo, Wis.

GINGER CUP CAKE.

Three cupfuls of flour, one cupful of sugar, one cupful of molasses, one cupful of butter, one cupful of sweet milk, three eggs, one tablespoonful of ginger, one tablespoonful of cinnamon, one teaspoonful of soda. Heating the molasses improves the cake.

Mrs. M. S. Bailey.

GOLD AND SILVER JELLY CAKE.

White part: Two cupfuls of sugar, one cupful of butter, one and one-half cupfuls of flower, whites of eight eggs, one teaspoonful of lemon. Yellow part: Two cupfuls of sugar, two-thirds cupful of butter, one and one-half cupfuls of flour, yolks of eight eggs. Put together in alternate layers with jelly.

Mrs. Comerford.

GOLD CAKE.

Yolks of four eggs, one cupful of sugar, one-half cupful of butter, one-half cupful of sweet milk, two cupfuls of flour, two teaspoonfuls of cream of tartar, one-half of soda.

Mrs. Joel Pound.

GROOM'S CAKE.

One pound of butter, one pound of brown sugar, one pound of stoned raisins, one pound of currants, one and one-quarter pounds of flour, one and one-half pounds of chopped figs, one and one-half pounds of chopped blanched almonds, one pound of citron sliced very thin, eight eggs, one-half cup of molasses, one-half cup of sweet milk, three teaspoonfuls of baking powder, one nutmeg, one teaspoonful of cinnamon, one-half teaspoonful of cloves, two teaspoonfuls of lemon extract, two teaspoonfuls of vanilla, one-half teacup of brandy, cream the butter and sugar, add the eggs, well-beaten, put the baking powder in the flour, then rub the fruit in the flour, mix all well in a large dish stirring the spices into the mixture; add the brandy the last thing before baking. When you wish it extra nice, use a thin icing, then a layer of macaroons, then ice again, generously. It is a good plan to get the baker to bake this cake in a brick oven.

Mrs. Geo. C. Ginty.

HASH CAKE.

One and one-half cupfuls of sugar, one-half cupful of butter, one and one-half cupfuls of flour, one-half cupful of corn starch, one teaspoonful of baking powder, whites of six eggs. For filling: One cupful of raisins, one cupful of chopped hickory nuts, one-half cupful of currants, mix together with boiled icing, put on top and between layers. You can use figs and almonds if you wish.

Mrs. Waters.

HICKORY NUT CAKE.

Cream two-thirds cupful of butter, with two cupfuls

of sugar, add one cupful of milk, three even cupfuls of flour, three eggs, beaten separately, two teaspoonfuls of baking powder, one and one-half cupfuls of nuts, sliced fine, flavor with almond or vanilla. This is nice made in a loaf, or baked in dripper, with twenty-four halves saved for top. Frost and cut in squares.

Mrs. T. J. Cunningham.

ICE CREAM CAKE.

One cupful of butter, two cupfuls of sugar, whites of eight eggs, one cupful of sweet milk, two cupfuls of flour, one cupful of corn starch, two teaspoonfuls of baking powder.

Icing.—Whites of four eggs, four cupfuls of sugar, boil sugar in a little water until it begins to candy, pour this into the beaten whites and beat to a cream, add one teaspoonful of citric-acid to the frosting.

Mrs. M. S. Bailey.

KISSES.

Beat the whites of four eggs to a stiff froth, add three-quarters pound of sugar, flavor with lemon, butter your paper, drop the mixture—a small teaspoonful in a place—bake in a very moderate oven until the tops are hardened, slip them off carefully with a knife.

LEMON CAKE—No. 1.

One-half cupful of butter, two cupfuls of sugar, two and one-half cupfuls of flour, one-half cupful of corn starch, one cupful of sweet milk, six eggs, whites only, two teaspoonfuls of baking powder.

Filling.—Grated rind and juice of two lemons, two

eggs, one and one-half cupfuls of sugar, stir steadily over the fire until it thickens. When cold, spread between the layers. Mrs. Culver,

Bay City, Mich.

LEMON CAKE--No. 2.

Two cupfuls of sugar, two and one-half cupfuls of flour, one-half cupful of sweet milk, six tablespoonfuls of melted butter, six eggs, one teaspoonful of cream of tartar, one-half teaspoonful of soda.

Lemon Jelly.—The juice and grated rind of three lemons, two and one-half cupfuls of sugar, nearly half cupful of butter, six eggs; beat well together and scald until thick, and spread between layers. This makes a very large cake. Mrs. John Rumsey.

LOAF CAKE.

One cupful of butter beaten together with two cupfuls of sugar; add four eggs beaten separately, one teaspoonful of soda dissolved in one cupful of milk, two teaspoonfuls of cream of tartar mixed in three cupfuls of flour; flavor; beat well. This makes two loaves. Excellent. Mrs. L. H. Cushing.

LONG LAKE DOUGHNUTS.

One cupful of sweet milk, warmed with a piece of butter the size of an egg, three eggs beaten separately, one-half cupful of yeast, flour to make stiff enough to drop from the spoon. Let rise over night; in the morning drop the batter from the spoon on a well-floured board; let them rise half an hour, then fry in hot lard. When done, roll in sugar and cinnamon mixed together.

Mrs. Hollon Richardson.

MACAROONS—No. 1.

Whites of three eggs beaten to a stiff froth, one-half pound of cocoanut, one-half pound of rolled and sifted crackers, one teaspoonful of bitter almond, bake on a greased paper.

MACAROONS—No. 2.

One cupful of hickory nut meats pounded fine, one cupful of sugar, one and one-half eggs, two tablespoonfuls of flour.

MARBLE CAKE—No. 1.

For the white: One-half cupful of butter, one and one-half cupfuls of white sugar, one-half cupful of sweet milk, two and one-half cupfuls of flour, whites of four eggs, one-half teaspoonful of soda, one teaspoonful of cream of tartar. For the dark: One cupful of brown sugar, one-half cupful of butter, one-half cupful of molasses, one-half cupful of sweet milk, two and one-half cupfuls of flour, yolks of four eggs, one-half teaspoonful of soda, one teaspoonful cream of tartar.

Mrs. A. Hoffman.

MARBLE CAKE—No. 2.

Three-quarters pound of butter, one pound of flour, one pound of sugar, the whites of twenty eggs; mix in the usual way; take out one teacupful of the batter, mix well in it a tablespoonful each of ginger, nutmeg, cinnamon and allspice, teaspoonful each of mace and cloves. Put about half of the white batter into the cake pan, then put in the dark batter, then the rest of the white and bake.

Mrs. S. W. Chinn.

MIKADO CAKE.

One-half cupful of butter, one cupful of pulverized sugar, one-half cupful of water, one cupful of flour (measured before sifting), one-half cupful of corn starch, one teaspoonful of soda, two teaspoonfuls of cream of tartar, whites of four eggs. Cream the butter and sugar, add the water, then the corn starch and flour sifted with the soda and cream of tartar, and lastly the whites of the eggs beaten to a stiff froth, and stirred in lightly. Bake in three layers. For the filling: One cupful of raisins, chopped fine, one-half cupful of hickory-nut meats, chopped fine, yolks of three eggs, a pinch of salt, one cupful of sugar, and about one-third of a cupful of water; boil sugar and water until syrup threads, then pour it over the beaten yolks and the other ingredients, stirring well. Be sure that the raisins are plump and good quality. Mrs. T. L. HALBERT,
Montana.

MOLASSES COOKIES.

One cupful of molasses, one cupful of sugar, one egg, one cupful of butter, one tablespoonful of vinegar, one tablespoonful of soda, seven cups of flour.
Mrs. JAMES COMERFORD.

MOLASSES FRUIT CAKE.

One cupful of butter, one cupful of brown sugar, one cupful of sweet milk, three-fourths of a cupful of molasses, three cupfuls of flour, four eggs, one and one-half teaspoonfuls of cream of tartar, one teaspoonful of soda, two pounds of currants or raisins, chopped, one-third of a nutmeg, a little brandy; bake slowly.
Mrs. ELIZABETH PATTON.

MOTHER'S LITTLE CAKES.

One and one-half cupfuls of sugar, one-half cupful of butter, two eggs, three-quarters cupful of sour milk, one and one-half cupfuls of chopped raisins, one-half teaspoonful of soda, two cupfuls of flour before sifting, bake in gem tins.   Mrs. R. B. CLARK.

MOUNTAIN CAKE.

One cupful of butter, two cupfuls of sugar, one cupful of sour cream, four cupfuls of flour, six eggs, one teaspoonful of soda, two teaspoonfuls of cream of tartar.

Mrs. HIMMELSBACH.

NEAPOLITAN CAKE.

Black part: One cupful of butter, two cupfuls of brown sugar, one cupful of molasses, one cupful of strong coffee, four and one-half cupfuls of sifted flour, four eggs, two teaspoonfuls of soda, two teaspoonfuls of cinnamon, two teaspoonfuls of cloves, one teaspoonful of mace, one pound of raisins, one pound of currants, one-fourth pound of citron; bake the cake in round pans with straight sides; the loaves should be one and one-half inches in thickness after baked. White part: Whites of eight eggs, two cupfuls of sugar, two cupfuls of sifted flour, one cupful of corn starch, one cupful of butter, one cupful of milk, two teaspoonfuls of baking powder, flavor slightly with bitter almonds, bake in same pans as black cake. This makes two cakes. After the cake is cold, each black cake should be spread with a thick coating of lemon and sugar made as follows: Frosting: White of one egg thoroughly beaten, the grated rind of two and the juice of three lemons, and powdered sugar enough to make a thick frosting; then lay each white loaf upon each black one and frost as you would any other cake, being particular to use no other flavoring than lemon.

Mrs. T. J. Cunningham.

NUT CAKE, OR WHITE FRUIT CAKE.

Three-fourths of a cupful of butter, two cupfuls of sugar, one cupful of sweet milk, two and one-half cupfuls of flour, two teaspoonfuls of baking powder, four eggs, beaten separately, one-half cupful of corn starch, or one-half cupful more of flour, mixed with the baking powder, one cupful of stoned raisins, one cupful of walnuts, one-fourth pound of citron, flavor with almond; bake slowly in a deep tin one hour. In putting in raisins and nuts, mix with a little flour to prevent them from falling to the bottom.

Mrs. A. J. McGilvray.

ORANGE CAKE—No. 1.

One cupful of sugar, one and one-half cupfuls of flour, two eggs, one-half cupful of sweet milk, butter size of an egg, two teaspoonfuls of baking powder.

Filling.—One-half cupful of water, small half-cupful of sugar, butter the size of a hickory nut, two eggs, the white of one saved for frosting, small teaspoonful of corn starch. Mix the sugar and corn starch together, beat the yolks and add to the sugar and the grated rind of the orange, add the hot water and butter, and cook until it thickens; when done, add the juice of the orange, and the beaten white of the egg.

Mrs. J. W. Squires.

ORANGE CAKE—No. 2.

One cupful of melted butter, three cupfuls of sugar, four and one-half cupfuls of flour, one cupful of milk, one teaspoonful of soda, two cream of tartar, six eggs; separate the eggs.

Filling.—One pound of sugar, whites of four eggs, the rind and juice of two oranges; save enough of the icing for the top before putting in the orange; let the cake get partly cold before putting together.

Mrs. John Rumsey.

ORANGE CAKE—No. 3.

Two small cupfuls of flour, two small cupfuls of sugar, small half-cupful of water, yolks of four eggs and whites of two, juice and grated rind of one orange, two teaspoonfuls of baking powder; bake in layers and put together with any orange filling.

Mrs. John Robinson,
Green Bay, Wis.

PINEAPPLE CAKE.

One cupful of butter, two cupfuls of sugar, three of flour, four eggs, one cupful of milk, three scant teaspoonfuls of baking powder, leave out the white of one egg for the iceing, bake in layers and spread grated pineapple between, take the pineapple out with a spoon and do not use all of the juice; ice the top and sides with boiled iceing. Mrs. C. P. Barker.

PORK CAKE.

One cupful of pork chopped fine, one cupful of boiling water poured over it, two cupfuls of sugar, one egg, one teaspoonful of soda, three cupfuls of flour, one teaspoonful of cloves, two teaspoonfuls of cinnamon, one teaspoonful of allspice, as much fruit as you like; is better the older it is, if kept moist.

Mrs. W. H. Howieson.

POUND CAKE.

One pound of butter, one pound of sugar, one pound of flour, ten eggs; flavor with almond. This cake is improved by two tablespoonfuls of sweet cream.

Mrs. T. H. Grist.

PRINCE OF WALES.

Dark part: One cupful of brown sugar, one-half cupful of butter, one-half cupful of sour milk, two cupfuls of flour, one cupful of chopped raisins, one teaspoonful of soda dissolved in a little warm water, one tablespoonful of molasses, yolks of three eggs, one teaspoonful of cinnamon, one-half teaspoonful of cloves, one nutmeg. White part: One cupful of flour, one-half cupful of corn starch, one-half cupful of sweet milk, one-half cupful of butter, one cupful of white sugar, one large teaspoonful of baking powder, whites of three eggs. Bake in layers, and put together with iceing. Mrs. Piper,

Eau Claire, Wis.

PRUNE CAKE.

One and one-half cupfuls of sugar, one cupful of milk, one-half cupful of butter, three small teaspoonfuls of baking powder, whites of three eggs, nearly three cupfuls of flour. Bake in two or three layers.

Filling.—One-half pound fresh prunes, one-half

pound of seeded raisins, nearly one-half pound of figs. Steam the prunes so you can remove the pits; chop all together; add the pulp and rind of a lemon, two table-spoonfuls of sugar beaten with the yolks of three eggs; let this warm in a steamer so it will stick together, then spread between the layers and frost the top.

Mrs. H. Darland,

New Jersey.

QUEEN'S CAKE.

One cupful of butter, two cupfuls of sugar, four and one-half or five cupfuls of flour (sometimes flour varies), three eggs, three tablespoonfuls of sour milk, one teaspoonful of soda. Stir as little as possible; roll out and cut into thin cakes, brush over with beaten egg, and bake quickly. Mrs. F. C. Arms,

Pittsfield, Mass.

RAISIN CAKE.

One cupful of butter, one cupful of molasses, one cupful of sour milk, two cupfuls of sugar, six cupfuls of flour, one cupful of raisins, one teaspoonful of soda, three eggs, cloves, nutmeg and cinnamon to taste.

Mrs. T. M. Cary.

ROLL JELLY CAKE.

Five eggs, two cupfuls of sugar, two cupfuls of flour, one-half cupful of milk, two teaspoonfuls of cream of tartar, one teaspoonful of soda. Bake in square tins, spread with jelly, and roll while warm. This makes four rolls. Mrs. John Rumsey.

SAND TARTS.

Two-thirds teacupful of butter, one and one-half

teacupfuls of sugar, two eggs, one-half teaspoonful of soda, three teaspoonfuls of water, flour to make stiff enough to roll thin; brush the tops with the white of an egg, and sprinkle on sugar.   Will keep four months.

Mrs. H. H. Todd.

SILVER CAKE.

Four eggs, beaten separately, seven tablespoonfuls of melted butter, three and one-half cupfuls of flour, two cupfuls of sugar, two teaspoonfuls of cream of tartar, one of soda.   Mrs. Joel Pound.

SIX MONTHS' CAKE.

One and one-half cupfuls of butter, two cupfuls of sugar, one cupful of molasses, one cupful of sweet milk, four eggs, five cupfuls of flour, one teaspoonful of soda, one nutmeg, two cupfuls of raisins, two cupfuls of citron. This makes two long bars.

Mrs. T. R. Morgan,

Binghamton, N. Y.

SNOW CAKE—No. 1.

Three-fourths cupful of butter, two cupfuls of sugar, one cupful of milk, one-half cupful of corn starch, two and one-half cupfuls of flour, one and one-half teaspoonfuls of baking powder.   Mix flour, corn starch and baking powder together; add to the butter and sugar alternately with the milk; lastly add the whites of seven eggs; flavor to taste.   Never fails to be good.   Mrs. Wm. Irvine.

SNOW CAKE—No. 2.

One-half teacupful of butter, one cupful of sugar,

one and one-half cupfuls of flour, one-half cupful of sweet milk, whites of four eggs, one teaspoonful of baking powder; flavor with lemon. This is very nice baked in a loaf, cut in two and put together with boiled icing, and freshly grated cocoanut.

Mrs. H. F. Robinson.

SNOW-FLAKE CAKE.

Whites of ten eggs, beaten to a stiff froth, one and one-half gobletfuls of sifted flour, one gobletful of pulverized sugar, one-half teaspoonful of cream of tartar. Mix the sugar, flour and cream of tartar together lightly, stir in the beaten whites; flavor with lemon; bake in a slow oven. It is very nice if baked properly.

Mrs. W. L. Pierce.

SOFT GINGER BREAD—No. 1.

Two cupfuls of molasses, one cupful of sugar, one cupful of butter, one cupful of sweet milk, four eggs, two tablespoonfuls of ginger, nutmeg, four cupfuls of flour, full measure, mixed with three teaspoonfuls of baking powder. Bake in small tins. Excellent eaten warm. Mrs. H. H. Todd.

SOFT GINGER BREAD—No. 2.

One cupful of molasses, one-half cupful of lard or butter, one tablespoonful of ginger, one-half cupful of boiling water, one teaspoonful of soda.

Mrs. J. E. Dickinson.

SOFT GINGER BREAD—No. 3.

One coffeecupful of molasses (New Orleans), one teacupful of light brown sugar, one teacupful of sour cream, four teacupfuls of sifted flour, three tablespoonfuls of melted butter, one tablespoonful of ginger, one tea-spoonful of lemon extract, one teaspoonful of salt, two eggs, one-third cupful of sour milk, one teaspoonful of soda; bake in a small dripping pan in a moderate oven.

Mrs. L. C. Stanley.

SPICE CAKE—No. 1.

One coffee cupful of brown sugar, one tablespoonful of butter, one cupful of sour cream, two eggs, one tea-spoonful of soda, two cupfuls of sifted flour, one cupful of chopped raisins, one tablespoonful of cloves, cinnamon and nutmeg each.

Mrs. Wm. Irvine.

SPICE CAKE—No. 2.

One cupful of sugar, two eggs, one-half cupful of sweet milk, one-half cupful of molasses, one-half cupful of butter, one teaspoonful each of cinnamon, cloves, nut-meg and allspice, one and one-half teaspoonfuls of baking powder, two and one-half cupfuls of flour. Make boiled frosting and stir in one cupful of seeded and chopped raisins; flavor with one-half teaspoonful of vanilla.

This cake is much nicer when made in three layers; use the same frosting to put between the layers.

Miss Briggs.

Milwaukee.

SPONGE CAKE—No. 1.

Four eggs, the white of one saved for frosting, beat thoroughly, two coffeecupfuls of sugar, two coffeecupfuls of flour (after it is sifted), four teaspoonfuls of baking powder mixed with the flour, one cupful of boiling water the last thing before putting into the oven; bake immediately. This is very nice baked in layers with custard between.

Mrs. H. L. Cruttenden,
Northfield, Minn.

SPONGE CAKE—No. 2.

The yolks of four eggs, beaten with one even cupful of sugar ten minutes, one even cupful of flour, one-half teaspoonful of baking powder, and lastly add beaten whites of four eggs. Mrs. F. T. Condit.

STRAWBERRY SHORT CAKE.

Make a crust as you would for baking powder biscuits, only use more shortening, divide your dough, roll out half of it and put in your pan, melt some butter and spread over the top, roll out the other half and put in the pan; when your cake is done the top half will slip from the other if you have buttered it sufficiently; spread with more butter, have your berries mashed and sweetened, put them between the cakes and return to the oven a few minutes; pour cream over just before serving, or have cream on the table and use when you serve.

SUGAR COOKIES—No. 1.

Two cupfuls of sugar, one and two-thirds cupfuls of butter, four eggs beaten separately, one teaspoonful of soda, two of cream of tartar, very small half cupful of milk, one teaspoonful of vanilla; mix soft; roll thin.

Mrs. L. F. Martin.

SUGAR COOKIES—No. 2.

Two cupfuls of granulated sugar, one cupful of butter, two eggs, two small teaspoonfuls of cream of tartar, one teaspoonful of soda, two large tablespoonfuls of sweet milk, little nutmeg; mix as soft as you can and roll thin.   MRS. WM. IRVINE.

SUGAR COOKIES—No. 3.

One and one-half cupfuls of sugar, three-quarters cupful of butter, three eggs, one-half cupful of sour milk, one-half teaspoonful of soda; flavor with nutmeg, roll thin, sprinkle with sugar, and bake.

ANNIE T. PETERSON.

SUNSHINE CAKE.

Yolks of eleven eggs, two cupfuls of sugar, one cupful of butter, scant the butter, one cupful of milk, one teaspoonful of cream of tartar, one-half a teaspoonful of soda, three cupfuls of flour. Flavor with vanilla. Three teaspoonfuls of baking powder may be used instead of the soda and cream of tartar; use with angels' food.

MRS. HIRAM ALLEN,

Bradford, Pa.

TAPIOCA CAKE.

Two cupfuls of sugar, two-thirds cupful of butter, one cupful of sweet milk, two cupfuls of flour, one cupful of corn starch, whites of six eggs, one and one-half teaspoonfuls of baking powder; bake in layers.

Filling for the above.—Five tablespoonfuls of tapioca soaked in water enough to cover, steam in the same water, adding more water when required, two-thirds cupful of sugar filled up with pink sugar sand; flavor with vanilla and spread between layers.

Mrs. J. C. Mitchell,
Chicago.

VERMONT CURRANT CAKE.

One and one-half cupfuls of sugar, one-half cupful of butter (scant), one-half cupful of sweet milk, two eggs, two cupfuls of flour, two teaspoonfuls of baking powder, one cupful of currants.

Mrs. H. L. Cruttenden,
Northfield, Minn.

VICTORIA CAKE.

Stir together to a cream, one and one-half cupfuls of sugar, one-half cupful of butter, then add one-half cupful of sweet milk, sift one and one-half cupfuls of flour, one-half cupful of corn starch, one teaspoonful of baking powder together; add the beaten whites of six eggs, flavor, bake in layers and put frost between and on top. This is very nice to use for any layer cake.

Mrs. Will Squires.

"WANDERING JEWS."

One and one-half cupfuls of sugar, one cupful of butter, two cupfuls of fruit, one-half teaspoonful of soda, one teaspoonful of cloves, one teaspoonful of cinnamon, one-half of a nutmeg, three eggs. Bake as cookies.

Mrs. Herbert Barker.

WALNUT CAKE—No. 1.

Two cupfuls of brown sugar, one-half cupful of butter, one cupful of sour milk, yolks of five eggs, one-half teaspoonful of soda put in the milk, two cupfuls of flour, one pound of stoned raisins, one pound of English walnuts, one tablespoonful of brandy, one teaspoonful of cloves, one-half nutmeg; bake in dripper. Save twenty-four halves for the top; frost with boiled frosting and put nuts on top; chop nuts and raisins, and put in the flour.   MISS FANNIE GINTY.

WALNUT CAKE—No. 2.

Two cupfuls of brown sugar, one-half cupful of butter, large measure, one cupful of sour milk, scant measure, yolks of five eggs, one teaspoonful of soda, two cupfuls of flour, one pound of stoned raisins, one pound of English walnuts, a little brandy or flavoring (extract of rose is very nice for this). Save twenty-four whole nuts for the top; break the rest fine into the cake ; one-half teaspoonful of cloves and nutmeg. This will make three dark layers.

White Layers.—Two cupfuls of sugar, one-half cupful of butter, whites of four eggs, well beaten, one cupful of sweet milk, three cupfuls of flour, three small teaspoonfuls of baking powder. This will make three layers. Also use boiled frosting between layers and for the top, made as follows: whites of two eggs well beaten, one and three-fourths cupfuls of pulverized or granulated sugar, water enough to dissolve the sugar, boil until it is ropy, when tried in cold water but not brittle. then stir it into the eggs gradually and beat until cold : put on the cake when it and the frosting is cold. This requires no flavoring with the nuts. Nice for company, as it cuts into so many pieces.   MRS. F. T. CONDIT.

WHITE LAYER CAKE.

One and one-half cupfuls of sugar, one-half cupful of butter, one cupful of sweet milk, two cupfuls of flour, whites of four eggs, three teaspoonfuls of baking powder, put together with milk frosting as follows: Two cupfuls of sugar, one-half cupful of sweet milk; boil from three to five minutes or until it will cream; beat until cool or put together with boiled frosting and fresh grated cocoanut.   Mrs. George B. Early.

WHITE SPONGE CAKE—No. 1.

One and one-half tumblerfuls of sugar, one tumblerful of flour, whites of eight eggs, two-thirds of a teaspoonful of cream of tartar.

WHITE SPONGE CAKE—No. 2.

Whites of ten eggs, one and one-half cupfuls of sugar, one cupful of flour, one teaspoonful of cream of tartar.

YELLOW SPONGE CAKE.

Yolks of ten eggs, one cupful of sugar, one cupful of flour, two teaspoonfuls of baking powder (piece of butter the size of a hickory nut improves it), sift the sugar, flour and baking powder into the eggs when well beaten, stirring all the time. A rose geranium leaf in the pan before putting in the cake gives it a good flavor; also in the white sponge cake.

Mrs. J. Rumsey.

—

FROSTINGS AND FILLINGS FOR CAKES.

BOILED FROSTING—No. 1.

One teacupful of granulated sugar, whites of two eggs, four tablespoonfuls of water on the sugar; boil

until brittle when dropped in water, beat the whites to
a stiff froth and pour the sugar slowly over the eggs,
beating all the time until cold; flavor.

Mrs. L. H. Cushing.

BOILED FROSTING—No. 2.

One cupful of sugar, four tablespoonfuls of water:
boil until it hairs; have ready the well-beaten white of
an egg: pour over the hot sugar and water, slowly
beating all the time.   Mrs. Geo. C. Ginty.

BROWN SUGAR FROSTING.

Three-fourths pound of No. 2 Muscovado sugar,
three-fourths cupful of cream or milk, butter size of a
hickory nut, put the ingredients together and boil
until it will harden in cold water, then beat until cold
enough to spread.   Mrs. R. B. Clark.

CARAMEL FILLING.

One cupful of maple sugar, one-half cupful of white
sugar, one-half cupful of cream; boil until it threads,
then stir until it is cool; add one teaspoonful of vanilla,
and spread on cake.   Miss Briggs,

Milwaukee, Wis.

CHOCOLATE FROSTING—No. 1.

Five tablespoonfuls of grated chocolate, one egg,
one cupful of sugar, one-half cupful of cream; beat the
egg separately; stir all together and cook until a thick
syrup, stirring until cold enough to put on cake.

Mrs. A. J. McGilvray.

CHOCOLATE FROSTING—No. 2.

Whites of two eggs, one and one-half cupfuls of powdered sugar, six tablespoonfuls of grated chocolate, one teaspoonful of vanilla; put the chocolate and six tablespoonfuls of the sugar in a sauce pan with two spoonfuls of hot water; stir over a hot fire until smooth and glossy; have ready the whites beaten to a stiff froth, and add all the sugar and the chocolate; stir well together and spread on the cake.   Ed. Cary.

CHOCOLATE FROSTING—No. 3.

One cupful of brown sugar, one-half cake of sweet chocolate, one-half cupful of sweet milk, butter size of an egg, two teaspoonfuls of vanilla; mix thoroughly and cook as syrup; let it cool and spread on cake as soon as taken from the oven.

Mrs. Comerford.

CUSTARD FOR ORANGE CAKE.

One and one-half cupfuls of sugar, whites of two eggs, juice of two oranges and grated rind of one, mix the sugar and the juice of the oranges together; if not juice enough to dissolve the sugar, add water; boil briskly until it ropes or threads when dropped from the end of the spoon, pour it over the beaten whites of the eggs as in boiled frosting; add the grated rind; when cool, put between any white layer cake.

Mrs. Waters.

FIG PASTE FOR CAKE.

Two cupfuls of sugar with just enough water to dissolve, boil till quite a thick syrup, then add while hot the whites of two eggs beaten very stiff, chop one pound of figs very fine, and stir into egg and syrup.

FILLING FOR LAYER CAKE.

One cupful of raisins, seeded and chopped, one cupful of almonds chopped, one cupful of figs chopped, mix all together and spread on boiled frosting between layers.

LEMON FILLING FOR CAKE.

One lemon grated, one cupful of sugar, yolks of two eggs, boil and let cool, mix with the whites of two eggs well beaten.

LEMON STOCK.

Four lemons, four eggs, one and one-half pounds of white sugar, one-half pound of butter; grate the rind and squeeze the juice of the lemons into a basin; put these two ingredients into a lined sauce pan with the sugar and butter. When all are nicely melted, beat the eggs well and add them to it; boil for about five minutes. Be sure you don't let the other ingredients boil before you add the eggs or it will be spoiled; put in cans and cover closely. It is ready at any time for lemon cake, to spread between layers. Will keep good one year.   Mrs. L. H. Cushing.

MAPLE SUGAR FROSTING.

Two-thirds cupful of maple sugar, cook to a thick syrup, pour over the beaten white of an egg. Beat until cold; no flavoring.   Mrs. W. E. McCord.

MILK FROSTING.

One and one-half cupfuls of granulated sugar, one-half cupful of milk; boil about five minutes slowly or until it will string from the spoon; then pour in a deep earthen dish and stir with a silver spoon until it is of the right consistency to spread over the cake. Just before you put it over the cake, add one-half teaspoonful of flavoring. Mrs. M. S. Bailey.

RAISIN FROSTING.

Make boiled frosting and stir in one cupful of seeded and chopped raisins; flavor with one-half teaspoonful of vanilla. Miss Briggs.

RAISIN MASH FOR LAYER CAKES.

One cupful of raisins seeded and chopped, one-half pound of pulverized sugar, whites of three eggs, beaten to a stiff froth; mix all together and spread on cakes.

PUDDINGS AND SAUCES.

ALMOND PUDDING.

Put over the fire one quart of milk, one cupful of white sugar, one cupful of almonds, blanched and chopped very fine (one pound of hard shelled almonds will make one cupful); when ready to boil, add one cupful of common starch dissolved in a little cold milk, let the whole boil three minutes, take from stove and stir in immediately the whites of seven eggs beaten to a stiff froth, turn into molds and put away until wanted. To be eaten cold with wine and jelly. Beat the jelly and thin it with wine. This pudding will keep several days in cool weather.   Mrs. A. E. Comerford.

APPLE PUDDING—No. 1.

Make a nice rich biscuit dough and roll out about half an inch thick, line a pudding dish with the same, then a layer of apples, bits of butter, sugar and nutmeg, then a layer of dough, then of apples, etc., and lastly of dough; steam two and one-half hours.

Miss Mary E. Bate,
Drywood, Wis.

APPLE PUDDING—No. 2.

Peel and slice sour apples, put a layer in your dish, sprinkle sugar, a little cinnamon, and put small pieces of butter over them; then put a layer of bread crumbs, another of apples, and so on until your dish is filled; bake until apples are done. Serve with whipped cream.   Mrs. M. S. BAILEY.

APPLE TAPIOCA PUDDING.

To one-half teacupful of tapioca, add one and one-half pints of cold water; let it stand on stove until cooked clear (stirring to prevent burning), remove, sweeten and flavor with nutmeg and one wine glassful of wine, pour the tapioca into a deep dish, in which have been placed six or eight pared and cored apples; bake until apples are done and serve cold with cream.

Mrs. D. G. COLEMAN.

BIRD'S NEST PUDDING.

Put the apples pared and cored in a deep dish buttered, fill the center of the apple with butter, sugar and cinnamon. Put in oven and bake until nearly done, then pour over the apples a batter made of one quart of milk, eight tablespoonfuls of flour and eight eggs, finish the baking and eat with wine sauce or sugar and cream.

BROWN BATTER PUDDING.

One cupful of molasses, one cupful of sweet milk, three cupfuls of sifted flour, one cupful of raisins, one of currants, two eggs, a small piece of butter, a little nutmeg and salt, one-half teaspoonful of soda. Boil in a tin mold well-greased; the batter must not quite fill the mold, and the water in the kettle must not quite reach the top of the mold; boil three hours without stopping.

Sauce.—One cupful of sugar, three-fourths of a cupful of butter, one pint of boiling water; beat the butter and sugar together to a foam, then add boiling water; flavor with lemon or vanilla. MRS. T. M. CARY.

BATTER PUDDING.

Four eggs, eight tablespoonfuls of flour, one pint of sweet milk, a little salt, add one teaspoonful of baking powder. Steam one hour.

BOILED RICE.

Boil one cupful of rice until quite soft, sweeten with sugar and pile up on a dish, spot it with lumps of jelly, beat the whites of three eggs with a little sugar, flavor with lemon or vanilla, and pour over the rice.

MRS. O. HOLT.

COTTAGE PUDDING—No. 1.

One cupful of sugar, one-half cupful of butter, one-half cupful of sweet milk, two eggs, one and one-half teaspoonfuls of baking powder, two even cupfuls of flour, and flavor with lemon. Bake. To be eaten warm, with liquid sauce.

COTTAGE PUDDING—No. 2.

One cupful of milk, two of flour, three teaspoonfuls of baking powder, two tablespoonfuls of melted butter, one egg, one small cupful of sugar. Steam three-fourths of an hour, and serve with the following sauce: One cupful of powdered sugar, one-half cupful of butter, beat to a cream, add a wineglassful of wine or brandy, stir thoroughly and put in sauce-tureen; pour in boiling water slowly. The sauce will look like cream, and foam.

MRS. W. LE CLERC.

CHOCOLATE PUDDING—No. 1.

Let one pint of milk come to the boiling point; add one-half cupful of sugar, two tablespoonfuls of grated chocolate, one large tablespoonful of corn starch; boil until thick; pour into a mold and place on ice; flavor with vanilla. Serve with cream and sugar.

Mrs. F. C. WEBB.

CHOCOLATE PUDDING—No. 2.

One quart of milk, ten tablespoonfuls of grated bread crumbs, four tablespoonfuls of grated chocolate, one cupful of sugar, four eggs (whites of two reserved for frosting), small piece of butter. Scald milk, bread, sugar, butter and chocolate together; take from fire and add eggs well beaten; bake one-half hour or more; beat the whites to a froth and add two tablespoonfuls of powdered sugar. Spread on top, put in oven, and brown slightly. Serve cold.

Mrs. H. L. CRUTTENDEN,
Northfield, Minn.

CORN PUDDING.

One quart of milk, one dozen ears of sweet corn. Cut the grains of corn half off and pound them well in chopping bowl; scrape the remainder from the cob and stir the whole well in the milk; add one teaspoonful of salt, one-half teaspoonful of black pepper, one-half teaspoonful of grated nutmeg, two tablespoonfuls of sugar, one-fourth pound of butter. Bake slowly for four hours.

Mrs. C. COLEMAN.

CREAM TAPIOCA PUDDING.

Soak three tablespoonfuls of tapioca in water over

night, then boil in one quart of milk half an hour, beat the yolks of four eggs with one cupful of sugar, add three tablespoonfuls of cocoanut, boil ten minutes longer, pour into a pudding dish, beat the whites of four eggs to a stiff froth with three tablespoonfuls of sugar, put over top and sprinkle with cocoanut; bake five minutes: eat cold. Mrs. F. C. Webb.

COOPERSTOWN PUDDING.

Mix three tablespoonfuls of flour, with one of corn starch in a little milk and stir into one pint of boiling milk; let it cool a little; add a little salt, four eggs (whites and yolks beaten separately), butter the size of an egg; bake in pudding dish in a pan of water; eat with sauce. Mrs. Daisy Grossman.

CREAM PIE.

For the cake, take butter the size of an egg, one cupful of sugar, two eggs, one-third cupful of milk, two cupfuls of flour, two teaspoonfuls of baking powder; bake in two tins for two pies. For the cream, take one pint of milk (taking out enough to wet one-half cupful of flour), boiled with two-thirds cupful of sugar and yolks of two eggs, add the flour to milk and boil three minutes; when cold, flavor with lemon or vanilla, and spread between upper and lower crusts of each pie after cutting them smoothly apart. To be eaten with whipped cream. Mrs. M. S. Bailey.

CHOCOLATE CORN STARCH.

Pour one pint of boiling milk over twelve tablespoonfuls of grated chocolate, add three tablespoonfuls of corn starch, three eggs well-beaten, one pint of cold milk, three tablespoonfuls of sugar, and one teaspoonful of vanilla to the melted chocolate; boil all together one minute, stirring briskly. Pour into molds and serve cold, with cream.

APPLE PUDDING.

Fill a medium sized pudding dish two-thirds full of sliced apples; cover closely and bake. When done, beat together the yolks of three eggs, one cupful of sugar, juice of one lemon, one teaspoonful of flour; add to this after it is well mixed the beaten whites, then pour over the apples and bake fifteen minutes. To be eaten with cream.   MRS. MOSES.

DELMONICO PUDDING.

Yolks of four eggs, one quart of milk, slightly sweetened, three tablespoonfuls of corn starch, bake ten minutes, beat the whites of the four eggs to a stiff froth, add one tablespoonful of powdered sugar to each egg. After the pudding has baked ten minutes, spread jelly over it, and on this the beaten whites of the eggs; set in the oven again, and bake until a light brown.
                                     MRS. D. G. COLEMAN.

ESCALLOPED APPLES.

A layer of chopped apples, a layer of toasted bread crumbs, a layer of suet chopped. Fill the dish, cover with milk and bake, eat with hard sauce made as follows: One-half cupful of butter, one cupful of sugar, one teaspoonful of vanilla, one teaspoonful of lemon, one tablespoonful of vinegar.   MRS. CLARA MITCHELL,
                                     Chicago, Ill.

ENGLISH PUDDING.

One pound of suet, two pounds of raisins, one pound of currants, one-half pound of blanched almonds chopped, one cupful of molasses, three eggs, three teaspoonfuls of mixed spices. Mix with flour and grated bread crumbs to the consistency of pound fruit cake ; steam four hours.

For Sauce.—One cupful of sugar, two tablespoonfuls of flour rubbed with one tablespoonful of butter, one pint of hot water, one pint of chopped butternut meats.

Mrs. Searles,

Stillwater, Minn.

ENGLISH PLUM PUDDING.

One-half cupful of sour milk, one cupful of butter, one cupful of suet chopped, eleven eggs, two and one-half cupfuls of brown sugar, one slice of citron cut in fine pieces, one gill of brandy, two teaspoonfuls of cinnamon, two of cloves, one-half teaspoonful of pepper, one of soda, two of cream of tartar. Stir in flour until it makes a stiff batter ; boil or steam six hours.

Sauce.—One gill of brandy, one cupful of sugar, one-half cupful of butter, one grated nutmeg, one pint of boiling water, thicken with flour.

Mrs. L. H. Cushing,

ENGLISH CHRISTMAS PUDDING.

(This is the old English plum pudding.) One pound of sugar, one pound of raisins, one pound of currants, one pound of suet, one pound of bread crumbs (powdered fine), one-half ounce of mixed spice, six eggs, one-fourth pound of mixed peel (take fresh lemon and orange peel grated and then mix), sufficient flour to bind the whole together with one-half pint of old ale or milk. Put it in a bag in boiling water and keep it boiling hard for four hours, make a sauce of wine, browned flour, butter, sugar and water and boil it. To use half of this receipt makes a good sized pudding.

MRS. DAISY GROSSMAN.

EASTER EGG PUDDING.

Make a mold of wine or lemon jelly in a round, shallow dish or pan the day before you want to use it. Take the rind of three or four oranges, cut them into shreds or straws, preserve them in sugar and water (that is, boil them in it until they lose all the bitter taste and are like preserves). Put this away to use next day with your jelly. Take a dozen or more eggs, make a small hole in the top, pour out the contents of the shells, and rinse them out thoroughly with cold water, set the shells into a pan of bran or corn meal and fill them up through the small hole in the top with gelatine "blanc mange." Make your "blanc mange" and dip out portions of it into cups or bowls; into some stir a little grape jelly, into another chocolate, into another a few drops of cochineal. The grape jelly will give you blue eggs; chocolate, brown; cochineal, pink, etc. Fill the shells with these mixtures and set away for use next morning. When you wish to serve the pudding, turn out the jelly upon a deep platter, put your orange straws on for a nest, peel the blanc mange eggs, rinse them quickly in very cold water, place in the nest and around the form of jelly. Eat with sugar and cream. Serve a piece of the jelly, a few orange straws and an egg or two on each plate; dust with sugar and pour cream over the whole.

Mrs. Geo. C. Ginty.

EGG PUDDING.

One quart of milk, six eggs, six tablespoonfuls of flour, a little salt, yolks and whites of eggs beaten separately; mix the flour with the yolks of eggs, heat the milk to boiling, then pour it on the eggs and flour, and lastly stir in the whites; beat well, and bake one-half hour. Mrs. H. H. Todd.

FARINA PUDDING.

One cupful of boiling water, sift in farina while boiling until a thick paste, take it from the fire and stir a few moments quite fast, then add one tablespoonful of hard butter, two eggs and a little nutmeg; butter the dish and pour this in with two cupfuls of milk; bake until done; serve cold with cream.

GENESEE PUDDING.

One quart of milk, one cupful of boiled rice, six eggs, one-half cupful of sugar, save the whites of three eggs and beat with one-half cupful of sugar to put on top. While it is warm, stir the rice, eggs and sugar into the milk; cook over a kettle of water like custard. To be eaten cold. Mrs. G. I. Brooks,

Bloomer, Wis.

GERMAN TRIFLE.

Put a pint of strawberries, or any other fresh fruit,

in the bottom of a glass dish ; sugar the fruit, put over it a layer of macaroons and pour over it a custard made of a quart of milk and the yolks of eight eggs beaten. Sweeten to taste; when cold place on top the whites of the eggs beaten to a stiff froth, with a little sugar, or whip cream to a froth. The whites of eggs may be ornamented by beating currant jelly with part of it, and putting it in alternate hills of white and pink.

Mrs. O. Holt.

HOWARD PUDDING.

One quart of milk : while that is boiling mix four tablespoonfuls of flour with cold milk until free from lumps; when the milk is boiling, stir the flour in with one cupful of sugar and one-half cupful of butter. When all is well mixed, take off and let cool, then add six eggs, one teaspoonful of lemon, and one cupful of raisins. Bake in deep dish two hours.

Mrs. Searles,
Stillwater, Minn.

INDIAN MEAL PUDDING—No. 1.

One quart of sweet milk, one large tablespoonful of butter, four eggs, well-beaten, one cupful of corn meal, one cupful of sugar, scald milk and stir in the meal when boiling. When cool add the rest, and bake.

Mrs. H. H. Todd.

INDIAN MEAL PUDDING—No. 2.

Boil one quart of sweet milk, mix in it two and one-half gills of corn meal very smoothly, seven eggs well-beaten, one gill of molasses and a good piece of butter. Bake two hours.   Virginia Cook Book.

JOHN'S DELIGHT.

One cupful of bread crumbs, one-quarter cupful of chopped suet, one-fourth cupful of molasses, one egg, one-half cupful of seeded raisins, one-half cupful of sweet milk, with one-fourth teaspoonful of soda dissolved in it, one-fourth teaspoonful of cloves, one-half teaspoonful of cinnamon. Boil one hour.

Sauce.—Beat one-fourth cupful of butter to a cream, add one cupful of granulated sugar, and stir until it is white and foaming. Just before serving, pour on it one-third cupful of boiling water and stir a moment; flavor with wine or anything you prefer. Miss E. A. C.

LEMON RICE PUDDING.

One quart of milk, one heaping cupful of boiled rice, two cupfuls of sugar, five eggs, two lemons, grate rind and juice of one lemon, put into pudding with one cupful of sugar, yolks of five eggs and white of one. Bake one-half hour.

For Frosting.—Beat the four remaining whites stiff; add one cupful of sugar and juice of one lemon; spread over the pudding when baked, and brown slightly in the oven. Serve cold. Mrs. T. M. Cary.

LEMON PUDDING.

One cupful of sugar, butter the size of an egg, one lemon, two eggs, six small crackers (powdered), nearly a pint of milk; beat butter and sugar together; add juice and grated rind of lemon, then eggs and crackers, lastly milk. Bake half an hour.

Mrs. A. Hoffman.

LEMON PUFFS.

One pint of sweet milk, five tablespoonfuls of flour, one tablespoonful of melted butter, six eggs, leaving out whites of three. Bake in buttered earthen cups half filled, twenty minutes.

Sauce.—One large cupful of sugar, one-half cupful of butter, one egg, one lemon, all of the juice and one-half of the grated peel, one small nutmeg, three tablespoonfuls of boiling water: cream the butter and sugar, stir in the egg whipped light, the lemon and nutmeg, beat ten minutes, add (spoonful at a time) the boiling water. Place the bowl in top of teakettle, which must be kept boiling until the steam heats the sauce very hot, but not boiling; stir constantly.

Do not wash your cups, but wipe with a coarse cloth, keep them for these puffs.

Mrs. H. O. CRANE,

Green Bay, Wis.

LEMON PUDDING.

Four eggs, the weight of three in Indian meal, one-half pound of sugar, one-fourth pound of butter, one lemon grated, one small teacupful of sweet milk, two teaspoonfuls of baking powder sifted in with the meal; stir butter and sugar to a cream; beat eggs separately, then add lemon and meal; bake one hour. Serve with sugar and cream.

NOTTINGHAM PUDDING.

One pint of milk, two eggs well beaten, one scant pint of flour, a little salt. Place apples, pared and cored, in a pudding dish; pour batter over them and bake one hour. Eat with a sauce.

ORANGE PUDDING.

Peel and slice six oranges and sprinkle over them one cupful of white sugar. Let stand two or three hours; put a pint of milk in a tin pail and set in a kettle of hot water until it comes to a boil. Beat the yolks of three eggs with three tablespoonfuls of sugar and one of corn starch; pour this in the hot milk and cook until thick. When cool, pour this on your oranges in your serving dish, and stir together; beat the whites of the eggs to a stiff froth, add three teaspoonfuls of powdered sugar, pour over the pudding, set in the oven in a dish of cold water until it is slightly browned over the top; to be eaten cold. Prepare a pudding in the same way and use canned peaches instead of oranges, and it is very nice. Mrs. J. Rumsey.

PUFF PUDDING—No. 1.

One cupful of sweet milk, thirteen tablespoonfuls of flour, four eggs; stir the yolks of the eggs into the milk; add the flour, beat the whites of the eggs separately and add them last. Sauce.—Butter, sugar and lemon beaten very light. Bake. Mrs. Daisy Grossman.

PUFF PUDDING—No. 2.

One cupful of milk, one cupful of flour, one egg, a little salt, bake in cups. Eat with sweetened cream.

PLUM PUDDING.

Pour a cupful of milk over one pound of fine bread crumbs, and let it stand half an hour: then beat in four ounces of sugar, one-half pound of suet chopped fine, one-half pound of chopped raisins, one-half teacupful of grated lemon peel. Beat all well, with four eggs, and boil five hours.   Mrs. L. H. Cushing.

PINEAPPLE PUDDING.

Prepare ripe pineapple by grating it very fine, make a custard with cream and egg, heat the custard over steam until sufficiently hot to congeal the cream (having drained the pineapple free from juice and sweetened it one hour before it will be ready to mix with the cream). Pour in a dish that has been heated, a layer of the cream, then a layer of the pineapple until the whole is in the dish; beat sweet cream stiff, sweeten very sweet, and just before the dessert is served add the juice of the fruit, and pile the beaten cream on top. Care must be taken or the custard and cream will get sour. Cocoanut pudding can be made in the same way.

Mrs. Daisy Grossman.

QUEEN OF PUDDINGS.

One pint of bread or cake crumbs, one quart of milk, one cupful of sugar, yolks of four eggs, grated rind of a lemon, butter the size of an egg. When baked, beat the whites of four eggs to a stiff froth, add one cupful of sugar and juice of the lemon, spread on the pudding, jelly or jam, then the frosting, and bake a delicate brown.

QUICK PUDDING.

Soften any kind of light cake with sweet cream or rich milk, heated and poured on hot, make a rich boiled custard and pour it over the cake and cream while hot, and beat the whole together well; flavor the same as cake, with lemon or vanilla. It can be eaten hot or cold. Use a sauce of butter and sugar beaten together until light. The pudding should be as thick as baked custard..

RICE PUDDING—No. 1.

One-half cupful of rice (not cooked), one cupful of sugar, three pints of milk, one-half teaspoonful of salt, one cupful of raisins; mix all together and bake in a slow oven, stirring occasionally. To be eaten hot or cold. Season with nutmeg. MRS. A. HOFFMAN.

RICE PUDDING—No. 2.

One cupful of rice, one quart of milk (swell the rice), then mix with milk, add two eggs, one-half cupful of butter, sugar, spice and raisins without rule; bake.

RICE MÉRINGUE.

One cupful of rice boiled tender. When cool, add the yolks of three eggs, one tablespoonful of sugar, one cupful of sweet cream, a little salt, the rind of one lemon grated. Bake in oven. Beat the whites of the three eggs to a froth, add one and one-half cupfuls of sugar and the juice of one lemon; pour on top and brown.
MRS. A. E. COMERFORD.

STEAMED BREAD PUDDING.

One bowl of bread crumbs, one cupful of cold water, one of molasses, one of flour, one of raisins and citron mixed, one teaspoonful of cinnamon, one teaspoonful of soda; steam one hour.
MRS. V. W. BAYLESS,
Minneapolis, Minn.

STEAMED PUDDING.

One cupful of sugar, one cupful of flour, four eggs, small teaspoonful of soda, two of cream of tartar. Beat eggs and sugar together. Put soda in half of flour and tartar in remainder. Will steam in half an hour.

STEAMED FLOUR PUDDING.

One pint of flour, one and one-half cupfuls of sweet milk, three eggs, a little salt, two teaspoonfuls of baking powder: steam three-fourths of an hour. Serve with hard sauce.   SUSIE C———

SWEDISH PUDDING.

One-half pound of flour, scant one-half pound of butter, one-half pound of sugar, eight eggs, a little salt; rub sugar and butter to a cream, add yolks, well beaten, then salt and flour, and lastly, whites of eggs, beaten to a stiff froth. Put the batter in cups and steam in a steamer one-half hour. Serve hot with strawberry sauce.

Sauce.—Scant one-half cupful of butter, one cupful of sugar, beaten white of one egg, one cupful of mashed strawberries: rub butter and sugar to a cream, add beaten white of egg, then strawberries, thoroughly mashed.   MRS. SEARLS,
Stillwater, Minn.

SUET PUDDING—No. 1.

One teacupful of molasses (New Orleans) one of sweet milk, one of chopped suet, three and one-half cupfuls of flour, one and one-half of raisins, one teaspoonful of soda, one and one-half of cinnamon, a little salt. Steam three hours.

Sauce.—One-half cupful of butter, creamed, with one

cupful of sugar, then add five tablespoonfuls of boiling water (one at a time); flavor with vanilla or brandy.

Miss NELLIE BRIGGS,
Milwaukee.

SUET PUDDING—No. 2.

One cupful of chopped suet, one of sour milk, one of molasses, one egg, three and one-half cupfuls of flour, one teaspoonful of soda, fruit and spice to taste. Steam three hours.

SNOW PUDDING.

One-third of a box of gelatine dissolved in one pint of boiling water (soak the gelatine a few moments in a little cold water), add two teacupfuls of sugar, put on ice until cold, then stir in the juice of two lemons and whites of two eggs well beaten; place in a mold until hard. This is to be eaten with a custard made by using the yolks of two eggs and one whole one, to one pint of milk; sugar to taste; flavor with vanilla; boil until thick. Serve when cold.

MRS. B. E. REID.

SPONGE PUDDING—No. 1.

One cupful of flour boiled in one pint of milk, two-thirds cupful of sugar, butter the size of a small egg, five eggs beaten separately; mix the flour smoothly in the milk, and set the vessel in boiling water, stirring it until it seems sufficiently cooked. Beat the yolks, add sugar, butter, a little salt, and the whites of the eggs. Bake in a pan set in hot water, one hour. Eat when hot, with brandy or wine sauce.

KATE E. WILSON,
Winona, Minn.

SPONGE PUDDING—No. 2.

Four tablespoonfuls (well rounded) of flour, two tablespoonfuls of sugar (well heaped), one pint of milk; boil all together, add butter the size of an egg, and six eggs beaten separately. stir all together well and bake in a pudding dish set in a pan of hot water, one hour. Sauce.—Stir to a cream, one cupful of sugar, one-half cupful of butter, add by tablespoonfuls one-half cupful of wine.   Mrs. Wm. E. Tallmadge.

SPONGE PUDDING—No. 3.

One-half cupful of flour, one-quarter cupful of sugar, one-quarter cupful of butter, six eggs, one pint of milk; heat the milk to boiling, then add flour, sugar and yolks of eggs, well beaten together; remove from stove and add butter; lastly just before putting into pudding dish, stir in lightly the whites of eggs, beaten to a stiff froth. Set in a pan of hot water and bake three-quarters of an hour. To be eaten with wine sauce.
                          Mrs. B. E. Reid.

TAPIOCA PUDDING—No. 1.

Five tablespoonfuls of tapioca, one quart of milk, four eggs, eight tablespoonfuls of sugar; soak the tapioca in water two hours, beat the yolks of the eggs and sugar together, boil the milk, stir in the yolks of the eggs and sugar while boiling. then the tapioca, and stir until it begins to cream. Take out of the steamer into your baking dish, and flavor; set the baking dish into pan of hot water and bake twenty minutes; stir once while baking, beat the whites of the eggs with four tablespoonfuls of powdered sugar and spread over the top. Return to the oven a few moments.

TAPIOCA PUDDING—No. 2.

One quart of milk, four eggs, two tablespoonfuls of tapioca soaked one hour in cold water; sugar and vanilla to taste. Boil the milk and add a little salt, then stir in tapioca, sugar, yolks of eggs and vanilla; mix well and bake. Beat whites of eggs and a little sugar, and put on top. Bake to a light brown. Good eaten hot or cold.   Mrs. G. I. Brooks,
Bloomer, Wis.

TAPIOCA PEACH PUDDING.

Soak tapioca over night and in the morning boil until it is perfectly clear, adding more water from time to time as needed. Slice five nice peaches with a silver knife and sprinkle liberally with sugar. Take the tapioca from the stove, and stir the peaches into it. Eat cold with sugar and cream.   Polly M.

TAYLOR PUDDING.

One cupful of molasses, one of milk, three-fourths cupful of butter, six of flour, three eggs, two heaping teaspoonfuls of baking powder; steam three hours.

Sauce.—One cupful of butter creamed with two cupfuls of sugar, yolks of two eggs beaten very light, one cupful of boiling water. Just before serving put in the whites of eggs well beaten; flavor to taste.
Mrs. J. C. Mitchell,
Chicago, Ill.

TROY PUDDING.

One cupful of warm molasses, one cupful of sour milk, one teaspoonful of soda in milk, one cupful of suet, chopped fine, three and one-half cupfuls of flour, one cupful of raisins, chopped fine, one wine-glassful of brandy or wine, a little salt, one teaspoonful of cinnamon; steam three hours.

Sauce.—One tablespoonful of corn starch, made smooth in cold water; add one-half pint of boiling water, one cupful of sugar, one-half cupful of butter, yolk of one egg, well beaten, nutmeg, and wine or brandy.

TRIFLE.

Put in your pudding dish a layer of cake (pieces of all kinds can be used) then a layer of blackberry jam, then a layer of cake and so on until your dish is filled; put a few drops of brandy over it to flavor. To be eaten with whipped cream.

TIP-TOP PUDDING.

One pint of bread crumbs, one quart of milk, one cupful of sugar, the grated peel of one lemon, yolks of four eggs. Bake. When done, spread fresh strawberries over the top (or if not in season for them use a cupful of preserved raspberries), put over this a méringue made of the whites of the eggs, a cupful of sugar and the juice of the lemon. Return it to the oven to color; let it partly cool and serve it with rich cream.

WHOLE WHEAT PUDDING.

Two cupfuls of whole wheat flour (or sifted graham flour), one-half cupful of sweet milk, one-half cupful of molasses, one cupful of raisins, one-half teaspoonful of soda, one-half teaspoonful of salt; steam two and one-half hours.

Sauce.—Whites of two eggs, one cupful of sugar, one cupful of boiling milk, juice of one lemon.

Mrs. Walrath,

Cooking School.

WASHINGTON PIE.

One cupful of sugar, one-half cupful sweet milk, one-half cupful of butter, one egg, one teaspoonful of cream of tartar, one-half teaspoonful of soda, one and one-half cupfuls of flour; bake in two tins. For custard, take one cupful of milk or cream, one-half cupful of sugar, one egg, one tablespoonful of corn starch. Beat sugar, egg and corn starch together, and stir into the boiling milk and cook until thick; flavor to taste. Mrs. L. B. Cruttenden,

Cooperstown, N. Y.

PUDDING SAUCES.

WINE SAUCE—No. 1.

Rub to a cream one cupful of sugar and one-half cupful of butter, then stir in by teaspoonfuls one-half cupful of wine; set in a dish of hot water to dissolve.

Mrs. B. E. Reid.

WINE SAUCE—No. 2.

Take a lump of butter the size of an egg, and two tablespoonfuls of corn starch. Melt the butter and stir in the corn starch and add it to one pint of boiling water, one cupful of sugar, nutmeg, and wine or brandy to taste.   MRS. DAISY GROSSMAN.

NICE PUDDING SAUCE.

Three eggs and the white of one additional, one heaping cupful of sugar, beat eggs and sugar well together, take one cupful of boiling water and a piece of butter the size of an egg, let the butter melt in the water by setting it in the top of the teakettle. Just as you serve the sauce pour the liquid on to the sugar and eggs, stirring briskly; flavor to taste.

GOLDEN PUDDING SAUCE.

Take the yolks of three eggs, stir in one-half cupful of sugar, pour this into a pint of boiling milk, flavor with lemon, and set in a cool place.

MISS MARY E. BATE,

Drywood, Wis.

FOAM SAUCE.

One cupful of sugar, two-thirds cupful of butter, one tablespoonful of flour. Put it over the fire and stir in three gills of boiling water and one small teaspoonful of soda; flavor to taste.   MRS. H. H. TODD.

PUDDING SAUCE—No. 1.

Two cupfuls of powdered sugar, one cupful of butter, wine glass of wine, two eggs; beat all together one-half hour, and scald, not boil.

PUDDING SAUCE—No. 2.

Take two eggs, separate, and into the yolks put one-half cupful of white sugar. Beat very light, add three

tablespoonfuls of boiling water and beat again; flavor
to taste; lastly, add the whites beaten to a stiff froth.
and stir until ready to serve.

Mrs. C. M. Youmans,
Winona, Minn.

FOAMING SAUCE.

Whites of two eggs, one cupful of sugar, one cupful
of boiling milk, juice of one lemon.

EGG SAUCE.

Beat eggs, yolks and whites together thoroughly,
until smooth and creamy; sweeten to taste, and flavor
with nutmeg, wine, or any way you choose. This
makes a nice sauce to eat on any pudding.

Mrs. J. O. Ferris.

"AULD LANG SYNE."

A pudding receipt taken from "The Virginia House-
wife, or, Methodical Cook," published by Mrs. Mary
Randolph in 1831. Mrs. S. W. Chinn has a copy of
this quaint book, from which this receipt was taken:

BOILED INDIAN MEAL PUDDING.

Mix one quart of corn meal with three quarts of
milk—take care it be not lumpy—add three eggs and a
gill of molasses. It must be put on at sunrise to eat at
three o'clock. The great art in this pudding is tying
the bag properly, as the meal swells very much.

ICE CREAM, ICES, CREAMS, CUSTARDS, JELLIES, ETC.

ICE CREAM.

ICE CREAM—No. 1.

Two quarts of milk, one quart of cream, eight eggs, four teacupfuls of sugar, four tablespoonfuls of vanilla; beat eggs and sugar together (whites separately); steam the milk, add sugar and eggs, and let boil; then strain; let cool, and then add the cream whipped, and vanilla; then freeze.   MRS. L. C. STANLEY.

ICE CREAM—No. 2.

Three pints of milk, one quart of cream, eight eggs, two teaspoonfuls of vanilla, three cupfuls of sugar; let the milk come to a boil, stir in the sugar and yolks of eggs beaten well together; as soon as eggs are scalded take from the fire before it becomes thick; stir in the whites well beaten; when cold, add vanilla and small teaspoonful of salt; when half-frozen, add whipped cream.   MRS. M. S. BAILEY.

ICE CREAM—No. 3.

Two quarts of rich cream, one pint of white sugar, whites of five eggs, well beaten; flavor to taste; freeze.

MISS WILSON,
Menomonie, Wis.

ICE CREAM—No. 4.

Five pints of milk, five pints of cream, four and one-half cupfuls of sugar, whites of three eggs, two tablespoonfuls of gelatine dissolved in a little of the milk, four teaspoonfuls of vanilla, one even teaspoonful of salt: whip the cream, beat whites of eggs to a stiff froth, mix all together and freeze.

Mrs. A. Hoffman.

ICE CREAM—No. 5.

One quart of cream, one cupful of sugar, nearly one teaspoonful of vanilla; freeze.

Mrs. G. Tabor Thompson,
Eau Claire, Wis.

ICE CREAM—No. 6.

One quart of milk, one cupful of sugar, two table-spoonfuls of flour, one saltspoonful of salt, two eggs, one quart of cream, one-half to one cupful of sugar, one tablespoonful of flavoring; boil the milk; mix the sugar, flour and salt: add the eggs and beat all together; add the boiling milk, and when well mixed turn into double boiler, and cook twenty minutes, stirring constantly until smooth, after that occasionally; when cold, add cream, flavoring and sugar; make quite sweet.

May Williams.

CHIPPEWA ICE CREAM.

Two quarts of cream, two quarts of milk, two pounds of sugar; stir the sugar in the milk, add the cream; flavor to taste with vanilla: put in freezer, add the beaten white of one egg: then freeze.

Mrs. John W. Squires.

CHOCOLATE ICE CREAM.

To three pints of cream take one pint of new milk, two eggs, one teacupful of grated chocolate, two coffeecupfuls of powdered sugar, one teaspoonful of corn starch, and one of extract of vanilla; beat the eggs; stir them in the milk; add the corn starch and sugar; let them come to a boil; take them quickly from the fire; stir it all the time; when perfectly smooth, mix it with the eggs and milk; then add the cream and vanilla; if not sweet enough add more sugar; when cold, put in the freezer.

GREEN MOUNTAIN ICE CREAM.

To make three gallons of ice cream use the following: Five quarts of good milk, two and one-half quarts good thick cream, six pounds of granulated sugar, ten tablespoonfuls of the finest corn starch, six ounces of pure extract of vanilla.

Formula.—Boil milk twelve minutes in tin pail set into kettle of boiling water; now stir in corn starch and continue boiling six minutes; remove and stir until cold; next whip the cream until all lumps are out and it is perfectly smooth; put cream and cooked milk in freezer and stir thoroughly; then add sugar and stir until all is dissolved. Then flavor and it is ready to freeze.   F. P. HUNT.

PINEAPPLE ICE CREAM.

One quart of cream, one and one-quarter pounds of white sugar, one large pineapple, chop the pineapple and mix with the sugar; let this stand in a covered dish several hours; strain and stir into the cream slowly and freeze at once.   MRS. DAISY GROSSMAN.

ICES.

LEMON ICE—No. 1.

Three pounds of sugar, two quarts of water; boil sugar and water until clear, then cool; add the juice of six lemons and three oranges to the syrup; when half frozen add the whites of two eggs beaten to a stiff froth; then freeze hard.   Mrs. J. C. Outhwaite,

Depere, Wis.

LEMON ICE—No. 2.

One quart of water, one pint of sugar, juice of six lemons; mix all together and strain; then freeze.

LEMON ICE—No. 3.

Make a quart of nice lemonade, sweeter than to drink; add two grated oranges; strain and freeze.

Mrs. L. H. Cushing.

ORANGE ICE.

One quart of water, one quart of sugar, juice of four oranges and two lemons; strain and freeze.

Mrs. R. B. Clark.

PINEAPPLE ICE—No. 1.

One can of grated pineapple, one pint of sugar, one pint of water; pour over the sugar and let it dissolve; strain and freeze.   Mrs. R. B. Clark.

PINEAPPLE ICE—No. 2.

To one quart of grated pineapple, add one and one-fourth pound of sugar and one pint of water; beat the whites of two eggs to a stiff froth; add the above to the eggs little by little, beating well to make them mix; strain and freeze.

PEACH ICE.

One can or twelve large peaches, two coffeecupfuls of sugar, one pint of cold water, whites of three eggs, beaten to a froth; slice the peaches and stir all the ingredients together and freeze in form. Should be made night before using in order to freeze.

MISS LOUISA SMITH,

Ottawa, Ont.

LEMON SHERBET—No. 1.

One tablespoonful of gelatine, one quart of water, one pint of sugar, one tablespoonful sherry wine, juice of two oranges, juice of four lemons, grated rind of two lemons and oil of two lemons; strain and freeze.

MRS. WALRATH,

Cooking School.

LEMON SHERBET—No. 2.

One gallon of water, juice of one dozen lemons, the whites of eight eggs slightly beaten; sugar to taste; beat well and freeze.   MISS WILSON,

Menomonie, Wis.

ORANGE SHERBET.

One tablespoonful gelatine, one and one-half cupfuls of cold water, one and one-half cupfuls of boiling water, one cupful of sugar, six oranges or one pint of juice, one-fourth teaspoonful of vanilla; dissolve the gelatine in the boiling water; mix all together; strain and freeze.

FROZEN APRICOTS.

One can of apricots, a generous pint of sugar, one quart of water, one pint of whipped cream; cut the apricots into small pieces; add sugar and water, and freeze; when nearly frozen, add the cream.

CREAMS.
AMERICAN CREAM.

One-half of one-ounce package of Cox's gelatine put into one quart of cold milk; put in a tin pail; set pail in a kettle of cold water, and set kettle on stove; when the water has boiled two minutes, stir in the yolks of four eggs that have been beaten with four tablespoonfuls of sugar; then let remain in boiling water five minutes longer; meanwhile the whites of the eggs should be beaten to a stiff froth, and four tablespoonfuls of sugar added *after they are stiff*. Take the mixture from the stove, stir in whites of eggs, flavor with one teaspoonful of vanilla and one-half teaspoonful of lemon; put in mold; set in cold place. Serve with whipped cream. Best made the day before using.

GALLOWAY HOUSE,
Eau Claire, Wis.

BRANDY CREAM.

Heat boiling hot one quart of good rich cream, from previous night's milking; have ready three thoroughly beaten eggs; take the cream from the fire and stir in the eggs; dissolve loaf sugar, to suit taste, in one-half pint of French brandy; when cream is cold, stir in brandy and sugar; beat well and serve in glasses.

MISS WILSON,
Menomonie, Wis.

CHOCOLATE CREAM.

One quart of milk, four tablespoonfuls of chocolate

(that flavored in the vanilla, if you can get it), three-quarter cupfuls of sugar, six eggs, one pint of whipped cream, a saltspoonful of salt, one teaspoonful of extract of vanilla, a bit of soda. Heat the milk in a farina kettle with the soda and salt, wet up the chocolate with a little cold milk and stir it in; stir constantly until the chocolate is dissolved; beat eggs and sugar together in a bowl, pour the hot milk and chocolate on them, mix thoroughly and return to the fire, stirring well; when it is thickened nicely, pour it out, flavor and set away to get cold. Serve with whipped cream sweetened with pulverized sugar.

ITALIAN CREAM.

Sift three tablespoonfuls of ground rice, add it to two of powdered sugar and mix it smoothly with two of rose water, then stir in gradually a pint of cream and stir the whole over a gentle fire until of a proper thickness. Serve cold.   MRS. O. S. HOLT,

Rush Centre, Kansas.

MANIOC CREAM.

One pint of sweet milk boiled, soak one-half tea-cupful of manioc in cold water about half an hour, take two eggs, beat yolks, sweeten to taste, then stir yolks and sugar and manioc into the boiling milk; when thoroughly scalded remove from the fire and flavor to taste; then stir in the beaten whites of eggs. Serve cold with whipped cream.   MRS. W. CASWELL.

RASPBERRY CREAM BLANC MANGE.

Take the juice of one pound of berries (strawberries or raspberries), mixed with a good deal of sugar, a coffeecupful of cream, one ounce of gelatine, dissolved in a little hot water, and when luke-warm add it to the juice; then add the cream; stir very little; pour into a mold, and set on ice for two hours.

SPANISH CREAM.

One-half box of gelatine, three-fourths pound of white sugar, one pint of milk, one-half cupful of water, three pints of cream, three eggs; dissolve gelatine in cold water; whip cream; beat eggs and sugar; pour the milk and gelatine alternately over eggs and sugar; stir cream in lightly; stir often while stiffening on ice; flavor with vanilla.   Miss Wilson,

Menomonie, Wis.

TAPIOCA CREAM.

Two tablespoonfuls of tapioca soaked in milk over night; boil one quart of milk; add tapioca; add one cupful of sugar, beaten thoroughly with the yolks of three eggs; let it come to a boil; remove from fire; then add one teaspoonful of vanilla and the beaten whites of eggs; stir occasionally while cooling. Serve cold.   Mrs. Wm. Irvine.

VELVET CREAM.

One-half box of Nelson gelatine, one and one-half cupfuls of sherry wine, one lemon, grated rind and juice, one and one-half cupfuls of sugar, one and one-half pints of cream; soak the gelatine in the wine, add the lemon and sugar; heat all together until the gelatine is dissolved; strain, and set away to cool; when nearly cold (but before it begins to stiffen), add the cream ; beat until nearly stiff enough to drop from the spoon; pour into molds and set on ice until as stiff as Blanc Mange. COOKING SCHOOL.

WINE CREAM BLANC MANGE.

One pint of rich cream, one cupful of sugar, one teaspoonful of vanilla, two wineglassfuls of sherry wine, one-half box of gelatine ; dissolve gelatine in wine and whip the cream, add sugar and flavoring, and pour the wine slowly over the cream. Serve cold.

MRS. WM. O'NEIL.

CUSTARDS.

BAKED CUSTARD.

Scald, but not boil, one quart of milk ; add, by degrees, the beaten yolks of four eggs, and eight tablespoonfuls of sugar; when well mixed, add the whites of the eggs beaten to a froth ; flavor with nutmeg, and pour into a deep dish or cups. Set these in a pan of hot water, and bake until firm.

MRS. A. HOFFMAN.

BANANA CHARLOTTE.

This is simple and refreshing. The sides of a quart mold are to be lined with sponge cake and the bottom of the mold with thin slices of banana; fill the mold with stiff whipped cream ; set it aside in the ice-box until wanted. Remove carefully from the mold and serve.

CHAMPAGNE AMBROSIA.

Put a layer of sliced oranges in a dish, sprinkle a little sugar over them ; then a layer of sliced bananas, sprinkle with sugar; then spread a layer of cocoanut; repeat until dish is filled. Just before serving, pour a pint bottle of champagne over all.   MRS. G. C. GINTY.

CHARLOTTE RUSSE.

Dissolve one ounce of Cox's gelatine in one pint of warm milk; beat four eggs very light and add them to one pound of white sugar, which has previously been flavored with vanilla; when the milk containing the gelatine is cool, add to the other mixture. Have ready three pints of whipped cream and add the above to it; stir until it is well thickened, and cool in forms or in a large glass or fancy dish. If you choose you can line your dish with lady fingers or put macaroons in layers through it. Half of this is enough for any ordinary occasion. Cox's gelatine is the best for Charlotte Russe. A box of this gelatine contains one and one-half ounces. Take two-thirds of a box for this receipt.

MRS. G. C. GINTY.

COFFEE JELLY.

One package Cox's gelatine, soak two hours in large cupful of cold water, two cupfuls *strong* clear coffee, two of sugar, two of boiling water; put soaked gelatine and sugar together, cover closely half an hour; pour on boiling water; stir well; add coffee; strain and put into mold. Serve with whipped cream.

MRS. H. DARLAND,
Newark, N. Y.

FLOATING ISLAND.

One quart of milk, six eggs, two-thirds cupful of sugar, one teaspoonful of lemon extract. Scald the milk, and add a little salt; then beat the whites of eggs to a stiff froth, and lay it on the scalded milk in spoonfuls; let them stand a few moments to cook; then lay on a plate; after which add sugar, yolks and lemon to the milk; stir well together until scalded; then turn into a dish, and lay the whites of eggs on top.

LEMON JELLY.

One box of gelatine, two cupfuls of sugar, one quart of water, six lemons. A piece of stick cinnamon improves the flavor; put in while gelatine is dissolving. Dissolve the gelatine in the water; add sugar and lemons; heat until all is dissolved; strain. Put into a mold. Mrs. G. Tabor Thompson,

Eau Claire, Wis.

MANIOC JELLY.

One cupful of manioc, soaked one-half hour in cold water; then add another pint of cold water; set over the stove and let boil until clear. Flavor and put in molds to cool. Serve with cream and sugar.

Mrs. W. Caswell.

ORANGE CHARLOTTE.

One-third of a box of gelatine, one-third cupful of cold water, one-third cupful of boiling water, one cupful of sugar, juice of one lemon, one cupful of orange juice and pulp, whites of three eggs; line the mold with sections of orange or lady fingers; soak gelatine in cold water until soft, pour on boiling water, add sugar, and lemon juice strained; then add the orange juice and a little grated rind and the pulp; cool in a pan of ice-water; beat whites stiff; when orange jelly begins to harden, beat until light; add whites and beat until stiff enough to drop; pour into a mold when cold. Eat with whipped cream.

Mrs. E. Funke,

Oconto, Wis.

ORANGE CUSTARD.

Juice of six oranges, strained, and sweetened to taste; heat it over a slow fire until the sugar is dissolved; take off the scum. When nearly cold, add the yolks of six eggs well beaten, and one pint of cream or milk. Return to the fire, and stir until it thickens. Pour into glasses, and serve cold.

Mrs. Daisy Grossman.

ORANGE JELLY.

Pare and slice eight oranges, sprinkle over a little sugar; take one-half package of gelatine, pour over it a little cold water; when swollen, add one pint of boil. ing water and juice of two lemons and two cupfuls of sugar. Pour this over the oranges, and set away to cool-

Mrs. W. G. Yates,

Cleveland, Ohio.

TAPIOCA JELLY.

One cupful of tapioca, four cupfuls of water; let it stand over night; in the morning add one cupful of sugar. Bake until clear like starch; then add one-half cupful of currants or cranberries, well beaten in. Eat cold, with or without dressing. Cream and sugar is very nice. Mrs. H. Darland,

Newark. N. Y.

WINE JELLY.

One box of Nelson's gelatine, one pint of cold water. After the gelatine is dissolved, pour over it one pint of port, sherry or Maderia wine; add two even pints of boiling water, one large cupful of sugar, a little stick cinnamon, and the juice of two or three lemons. Let it heat through thoroughly; take from the fire, and strain into molds, or one large dish. Cut up into squares with a knife if you serve it in a large dish or in little glasses.   Mrs. G. C. Ginty.

MISCELLANEOUS.

APPLE MÉRINGUE.

Pare and core six apples; take one tablespoonful of water, one cupful of pulverized sugar, juice and grated rind of one lemon; fill the cavity made by the core with the above mixture; add a little butter to each apple. Cover the apples with the méringue (made of the beaten whites of three eggs, and three heaping tea-spoonfuls of pulverized sugar, well beaten together); put in the oven and brown. When cold, serve with whipped cream.

APPLE FLOAT—No. 1.

Steam apples and put them through the fruit press, and when cold sweeten to taste; add the white of an egg, beaten to a stiff froth. Whip all together, and eat with sweet cream.   Mrs. G. C. Ginty.

APPLE FLOAT—No. 2.

To one quart of apples stewed and well mashed,

add the whites of three eggs, well beaten, and four heaping tablespoonfuls of sugar. Beat together for fifteen minutes, and eat with sweet cream and nutmeg.

Mrs. M. S. Bailey.

ORANGE FLOAT.

Mix one quart of water, juice and pulp of two lemons, one coffeecupful of sugar; boil until sugar is dissolved; strain, and again bring to a boil; add four tablespoonfuls of corn starch, mixed in a little cold water. Stir and boil fifteen minutes. When cold, pour it over four or five sliced oranges and one can of pineapple, or any other fruit you like. Spread over the top the beaten whites of three eggs; sweeten and flavor with a few drops of vanilla, and over the top of the eggs spread thick, sweet cream, whipped to a froth.

Mrs. M. S. Bailey.

PRUNE SOUFFLE.

One-half pound of French prunes, whites of six eggs, twelve tablespoonfuls of powdered sugar; steam prunes until tender; chop fine; beat whites of eggs to a firm froth; stir in sugar; stir in very lightly chopped prunes. Bake in a quick oven five or ten minutes, and serve at once, with whipped cream.

Mrs. H. Darland,
Newark, N. Y.

RICE IMPERIAL.

One teacupful of rice, with enough milk to boil it soft; add sugar and vanilla to taste, and boil until well cooked; then add whites of three eggs well beaten, and let it stand until quite cold. Put half a package of Cox's gelatine to soak in a very little water. When well dissolved, mix all together the rice, gelatine, a large coffee-cupful of whipped cream, some sliced citron, and raisins, or candied cherries, and put in a mould and stand on ice three hours. Serve with a rich custard or cream.

Who can cloy the hungry edge of appetite
By base imagination of a feast?

RICHARD II.

PIES.

PIE PASTE—No. 1.

Three cupfuls of flour, one cupful of lard, one-half cupful of ice water; mix lard in flour with a knife: add water; mix as little as possible: roll thin.

PIE PASTE—No. 2.

One pound of the best butter, one pound of flour, one teaspoonful of salt, one cupful of ice water. By measure, use one quart of flour and one pint of butter.

PIE PASTE—No. 3.

One quart of flour, one-half pound of lard, sweet and firm, one-half pound of butter, one small teacupful of ice water.

FRENCH PUFF PASTE.

One pound of flour, three-fourths pound of butter, one egg (use the yolk only), ice water; chop half the butter into the flour; stir the beaten egg into half a cupful of ice-water, and work the flour into a stiff dough; roll out thin; baste with one-third the remaining butter, fold closely, roll out again, and so on until the butter is used up. Roll very thin, and set the last folded roll in a very cold place ten or fifteen minutes before making out the crust; wash with beaten egg while hot. This paste is very nice for oyster-*pates*, as well as fruit pies.

APPLE CUSTARD PIE.

One cupful of very tart apples, stewed and sifted, one cupful of sugar, two-thirds cupful of milk, two eggs, one tablespoonful of butter; flavor with lemon or nutmeg; frost or not, as you please; one crust. A very nice flavoring for this pie, or a custard pie, is to take the peel of an orange, boil it in salt and water while you are preparing the pie; then take out, mash very fine, and add to the pie.

CRACKER PIE.

One teacupful of cracker crumbs, broken rather coarse, two teacupfuls of boiling water, one and one-half cupfuls of sugar, and the juice and rind of one large lemon. Bake with two crusts.

CREAM PIE—No. 1.

Cover a pie-plate with rich crust, sift over the crust a thin layer of flour, cover the flour with sugar; then add cream and sprinkle cocoanut over all; repeat flour, sugar and cream. Bake. Grated lemon peel can be used instead of cocoanut for flavoring.

Mrs. J. E. Dickinson.

CREAM PIE—No. 2.

One egg, three tablespoonfuls of sugar, one pint of milk, large tablespoonful of flour; boil; flavor when cool and put in a baked pie shell; or use two yolks, frosting with whites.

CHOCOLATE PIE.

Two cupfuls of milk, one-half cupful of sugar, three eggs (two whites reserved), two tablespoonfuls of chocolate, boiled in milk; add sugar, salt, eggs; pour in the crust and bake; whip the two whites stiff with three tablespoonfuls of sugar; flavor with vanilla.

COCOANUT PIE—No. 1.

Put one teacupful of cocoanut into a coffeecup and fill it with sweet milk. Heat to boiling in a double boiler two teacupfuls of sweet milk; stir in two table-spoonfuls of flour, previously dissolved in a little of the cold milk; add butter one-half the size of an egg. When cool, add five eggs beaten with one cupful of sugar, and enough more milk to fill the pie; bake. This will make one large or two small pies.

Mrs. O. P. Smith,

Beloit, Wis.

COCOANUT PIE—No. 2.

Half a grated cocoanut, four tablespoonfuls of sugar, four eggs; add milk as for custard pie, and frost. Or, one pint of milk, two eggs, one-half cupful of prepared cocoanut; sweeten to taste; little salt.

FRUIT PIE.

Two cupfuls of sweet cream, one cupful of sugar, one cupful of chopped raisins, four eggs, reserving whites of three for frosting.

LEMON PIE—No. 1.

Juice and grated rind of one lemon, one small potato grated, one cupful of sugar, one cupful of water, three tablespoonfuls of flour, three eggs, reserving whites of two for frosting.   MRS. G. C. GINTY.

LEMON PIE—No. 2.

Slice one lemon fine into a cup, after removing the peel; then fill the cup with water; add one cupful of sugar, and one tablespoonful of corn starch. Bake with two crusts.   MRS. A. HOFFMAN.

LEMON PIE—No. 3.

Grated rind of two lemons, one cupful of sugar, four eggs (reserving the whites of two), butter the size of an egg; beat all to a cream, add lemon juice, and bake. Beat whites to a stiff froth, add three spoonfuls of sugar and spread on top; return to oven and brown lightly.   MRS. L. H. CUSHING.

LEMON PIE—No. 4.

The juice and rind of one lemon, one cupful of sugar, yolks of three eggs, one tablespoonful of butter, one of corn starch, one cupful of hot water; cook all together, bake crust, fill with the custard, and frost. Flour can be used instead of corn starch, if preferred.   MRS. A. HOFFMAN.

LEMON TARTS.

Two lemons, two cupfuls of sugar, one of raisins, two of water, three tablespoonfuls of flour, a little salt; prepare lemons as for pies; seed and chop raisins; mix all together and boil; place a crust in tart tins; fill with mixture and bake.

Tart Crust.—One cupful of lard, one tablespoonful

of white sugar, white of one egg, three tablespoonfuls of water; mix very lightly as for pie crust.

MOCK MINCE PIE.

One teacupful of grated bread or cracker crumbs, one teacupful of raisins, one and one-half teacupfuls of brown sugar, one-half teacupful each of molasses and vinegar, three cupfuls of hot water, butter size of an egg; spice to taste. Three pies. The syrup left from sweet crabapple or peach pickles is nice to use for these pies. Mrs. H. H. Todd.

MINCE MEAT—No. 1.

Five pintbowlfuls minced meat, one-half tongue, one pintbowlful of suet, ten pintbowlfuls of apples, four pintbowlfuls of boiled cider, one pintbowlful of vinegar, two pintbowlfuls of New Orleans molasses, four pintbowlfuls of sugar, four lemons, juice and rind, three tablespoonfuls of cinnamon, two tablespoonfuls of allspice, one tablespoonful of cloves, one nutmeg, one heaping tablespoonful of salt, one teaspoonful of pepper, three pounds of stoned raisins, three pounds of currants, one pound of citron, one cupful of brandy. If not moist enough, add water in which the meat was boiled. When baking, add a good teaspoonful of butter to each pie. Mrs. T. J. Cunningham.

MINCE MEAT—No. 2.

Take five pounds of lean meat, boil, chop fine, with three pounds of suet; seed four pounds of raisins, pick and wash four pounds of dried currents, slice a pound of citron, chop four quarts of apples; put in a sauce pan, with a tablespoonful each of ground cinnamon and nutmeg, a teaspoonful each of ground cloves, allspice, ginger and white pepper, with the juice of two lemons and two and one-half pounds of sugar; pour over all one and one-half quarts of cider, one pint of molasses and a teacupful of melted butter; let come to a boil: bake in a rich crust.   Mrs. E. C. McCord.

MINCE MEAT—No. 3.

Two bowlfuls of lean meat, four bowlfuls of apples, one bowlful of suet, one bowlful of currants, two bowlfuls of raisins, four bowlfuls of sugar, one bowlful of molasses, one bowlful of vinegar, one bowlful of boiled cider. one pound of citron, one nutmeg, three tablespoonfuls of cinnamon, two tablespoonfuls of cloves, one tablespoonful of allspice, three tablespoonfuls of salt, juice of two lemons. Boil all together.
                                    Mrs. Will Squires.

MINCE MEAT—No. 4.

Six pints of meat, chopped fine, twelve pints of apples, seven pints of vinegar, two pints of molasses, twelve pints of sugar, six pints of raisins, four pints of English currants, one-half cupful of brandy, two pints of suet or one pint of butter. two nutmegs, twenty tablespoonfuls of cinnamon; ten tablespoonfuls of cloves, ten tablespoonfuls of allspice. This will make five gallons.   Mrs. A. Hoffman.

MOLASSES APPLE PIE—(Yankee).

Slice tart-apples thin, sweeten with half New Orleans molasses and half brown sugar (about one-half cupful of molasses), a little butter, cinnamon, a pinch of salt, a teaspoonful of water and enough flour sprinkled over to thicken the juice; tuck the crust under very snugly and bake slowly at first. It takes longer to bake than with all sugar.

Mrs. F. A. A. ROBERTSON.

ORANGE PIE—No. 1.

Beat to a cream a teacupful of powdered sugar and one tablespoonful of butter, add beaten yolks of three eggs, then the juice and rind of two oranges, one teaspoonful of corn starch; beat all together; lastly, stir in lightly the whites beaten to a stiff froth. Bake with one crust. Mrs. F. C. ARMS.

ORANGE PIE—No. 2.

Milk for one pie, three eggs, one-half cupful of sugar, one tablespoonful of corn starch (large), one orange; save the whites for the top of the pie; beat the yolks of eggs; put in the one-half cupful of sugar and the juice and grated rind of orange; put the milk on the stove with the corn starch; let it come to a boil, then add it to eggs, sugar, and orange. Bake with one crust.

Mrs. B. D. VILES.

PIE-PLANT PIE—No. 1.

Stew the pie-plant, sweeten, add grated rind and juice of one lemon and yolks of two eggs. Bake and frost like lemon pie.

PIE-PLANT PIE—No. 2.

Mix one-half teacupful of white sugar and one heaping teaspoonful of flour together: sprinkle over undercrust; then add the pie-plant, cut up fine; sprinkle over this another one-half teacupful of sugar and heaping teaspoonful of flour. Bake in a slow oven three quarters of an hour.   Mrs. M. A. Lysaght.

PIE-PLANT PIE—No. 3.

Cut up your pie-plant, pour boiling water over it and let stand while you are preparing the crust; then pour off the water, and to each pie put one cupful of sugar, with an egg beaten in: add a piece of butter.

Mrs. A. J. Bate.

PEACH CUSTARD PIE.

Use one crust, halve the peaches and turn hollow side up; sweeten, beat together one egg, one tablespoonful sugar, pinch of salt, and add cream or milk enough to cover peaches. Bake. Canned peaches can be used.

Miss Jennie Lysaght.

RAISIN PIE—No. 1.

One-half cupful of raisins, seeded and chopped, one cupful of water, one cupful of sugar, one small tablespoonful of corn starch, yolks of two eggs, well beaten, grated rind of one lemon; boil, and afterwards add the juice of the lemon. Bake the crust first and fill; then put the whites of the eggs on top, after being well beaten with three spoonfuls of sugar; brown nicely.

RAISIN PIE—No. 2.

One cupful of raisins, cook as dried apples, one cracker, rolled fine, one cupful of sugar, for one pie; grate the rind and use the juice of one lemon for two pies.   Mrs. C. P. Barker.

RIPE CURRANT PIE.

One cupful of ripe currants, mashed, one of sugar, two tablespoonfuls of water, one of flour, beaten with yolks of two eggs; bake; frost the top with beaten whites of the eggs and two tablespoonfuls of powdered sugar, and brown in oven.

RASPBERRY PIE.

Open a can of raspberries, drain off two-thirds of the juice and put the remaining juice and berries into a plate lined with pie crust; sprinkle flour over the top, also little pieces of butter; put on your top crust and bake. When you can get black raspberries in the summer, put a bowlful of them in a crust, with a little sugar, and treat the same way.   MRS. GEO. C. GINTY.

SQUASH OR PUMPKIN PIE.

Two teacupfuls of boiled squash, one teacupful of brown sugar, three teacupfuls of sweet milk, three eggs, one tablespoonful of melted butter, one tablespoonful of cinnamon, ginger or nutmeg, as preferred; little salt. Makes two pies.

SOUR CREAM PIE.

One cupful of sweet or sour cream, two cupfuls of sugar, one cupful of raisins chopped and seeded, one egg, juice of one lemon—vinegar can be used instead. Bake with two crusts.   MRS. J. O. FERRIS.

PICKLES.

How camest thou in this pickle?—TEMPEST.

A great deal depends upon the vinegar in making pickles—buy the best cider vinegar the market affords. If your pickles show a white scum on the top, take them out of the jar, pick out the soft ones, wash the hard ones in cold water, and scald fresh vinegar and pour over them. If a chopped pickle shows a white scum, set the jar in water and thoroughly scald, by letting it stand for several hours in the scalding water on the stove. You may be able to save it, but if you have been made the dupe of patent vinegar, you will have to throw your pickle away.

CUCUMBER PICKLES—No. 1.

To a gallon of water add one cupful of salt; make it scalding hot, and pour over the cucumbers; strain off. Next day scald again, and pour over the cucumbers. Do this nine mornings. Wash the cucumbers; take enough vinegar to cover them; heat with spices to a boiling heat, and pour over the pickles. Lay sliced onions on top, if you like the flavor.

Mrs. J. C. OUTHWAITE,

Depere, Wis.

CHOW CHOW—No. 1.

One peck of green tomatoes, twelve large green cucumbers, six onions, two large heads of cabbage, six green peppers, two quarts of vinegar, three pounds of brown sugar, two ounces of white mustard seed, two tablespoonfuls of cinnamon, one of cloves. Chop the tomatoes, cucumbers, onions, peppers and cabbage fine; put them in a jar and mix with them a pint of salt; let them stand over night; in the morning, drain thoroughly; put the vinegar, sugar and spices into a porcelain kettle and let them come to a boil; pour over the pickles; add a few bits of horseradish; cover with horseradish leaves, and place a plate on top to weigh the pickles down.   MRS. J. M. BINGHAM.

CHOW CHOW—No. 2.

One gallon of best cider-vinegar, one-half pound of ground mustard, two large heads of cauliflower, picked apart, and soaked in salt and water (strong) over night, two quarts of small white onions, forty small cucumbers, cut in rings, one teaspoonful of curry powder; boil the vegetables in the vinegar and spices until tender; then skim out; boil the liquor down and pour over the pickles.   MISS WILSON,
Menomonie, Wis.

CHOPPED PICKLES.

One-half cupful of ripe tomatoes, chopped fine, two roots of horseradish, one cupful of salt, one cupful of white mustard seed, two tablespoonfuls of black pepper, two of red, five celery stalks, cut fine, three large onions,

a teaspoonful of mace, one of cloves, two of cinnamon,
a teacupful of sugar, one quart of cider vinegar.

Mrs. B. Himmelsbach.

CUCUMBER SALAD.

One dozen large ripe cucumbers, pare and chop
(taking out the seeds first) the size of a small bean,
chop also twelve large white onions, six large red
peppers, add a quarter of a pound of white mustard
seed and the same of black, one gill of celery seed, one
teacupful of salt; mix all together; hang up in a bag and
let it drain for twenty-four hours; put in a jar and cover
with cold vinegar. If you live away from market and
cannot get celery, a small teacupful of this pickle mixed
with meat or fish salad makes it very nice.

Mrs. G. C. Ginty.

ENGLISH MUSTARD PICKLE.

Equal portions of white cauliflower, very young
green beans, small cucumbers, and small white onions,
a few pieces of horse-radish, and two or three red
peppers; each must be boiled until tender (but not boiled
together), in salt water, not long enough to become soft.
Take one pound of Coleman's Imported English
Mustard and three or four quarts of vinegar, add a tablespoonful of sugar; boil in a porcelain kettle; put the
cauliflower, beans and other ingredients in and let them
boil a few minutes; skim them out; pour the vinegar,
mustard, etc., over them, and put in air-tight jars.

Mrs. H. H. Brown,
Menomonie, Wis.

GREEN TOMATO PICKLE.

Slice one peck of green tomatoes thin, and six onions; strew one cupful of salt over them, and let them stand over night; then drain. Take one quart of vinegar, two quarts of water; boil pickles in the mixture ten minutes. Then drain again. Take two quarts of vinegar, two pounds of brown sugar, two even tablespoonfuls of ground cloves, mustard and cinnamon, one teaspoonful of ginger, one-quarter teaspoonful of red pepper. Put all together and boil fifteen minutes.

Mrs. C. H. Smith.

MUSTARD PICKLE.

Separate cauliflower into nice little sprigs; put it into salt brine (strong enough to hold up an egg). Let it remain in the brine three days; take it from the brine and let it stand one day in fresh water. Do the same to as many white onions as you wish to pickle with it. To one gallon of vinegar add two pounds of brown sugar, and let them come to a boil; stir in one and one-half pounds of good mustard, previously made with cold vinegar. Place a layer of the cauliflower and onions in a jar; sprinkle them with whole allspice and pepper corns. Do this until the cauliflower and onions are all in; then pour over the boiling vinegar and mustard. Mrs. B. Himmelsbach.

PEACH PICKLE—No. 1.

Three pints of brown sugar to one gallon of vinegar; throw in a few cloves and pieces of stick cinnamon, and a few berries of allspice; let come to boil; put in the peaches and boil them until you can pierce with a straw.

Put them in a jar, pour over the syrup and cover closely. Steam crabapples and use the same syrup to pickle them.   Mrs. L. C. Stanley.

PICKLED PEACHES—No. 2.

Eight pounds of peaches, four pounds of white sugar, one quart of water, one cupful of vinegar, one small handful of stick cinnamon, half as many whole cloves; heat the vinegar, water and sugar, and skim; put in the spices, pare the peaches and put a few at a time into the liquor; cook until tender. Put them into Mason jars. Peaches can be taken from the liquor carefully and put into the jars: fill the jars with the hot liquor, and seal.   Mrs. A. Hoffman.

PICKLED PEACHES—No. 3.

Seven pounds of fruit, five of sugar, one of allspice and cinnamon (tied in a bag and put in the vinegar), one quart of vinegar; stick a few cloves in each peach and lay in a jar; boil the sugar, vinegar and spices and pour over the fruit while hot, three mornings in succession.   Mrs. R. D. Whittemore.

PICKLED CUCUMBERS—No. 2.

Wash and put into a stone jar: prepare a weak brine to cover them; heat in a brass kettle and pour over them; the next morning, drain off the brine and heat again, skimming it when it comes to the boiling point, and pour over cucumbers hot; continue to do this seven mornings, then rince off the pickles in clear water, wipe them and pack in a jar; throw over the top of them a few pieces of horseradish, cinnamon, cloves and green peppers; pour over the whole some good cidar vinegar heated to a boiling point.

Mrs. A. Hoffman.

PICKLED PEPPERS.

Take large green peppers, cut off the tops and remove the seeds; soak the peppers in strong salt and water over night; chop and season cabbage with salt and pepper; stuff the peppers with this; sew the tops of the peppers on; boil in vinegar until tender; put in a jar and cover with cold vinegar, adding a few pieces of horseradish.

Mrs. A. Hoffman.

PICCADILLI.

One peck of green tomatoes, sliced thin, put in a jar in layers, with salt freely sprinkled over each layer; let it stand over night; twelve large onions, sliced thin: drain the tomatoes dry by squeezing the brine out with your hands; have ready all kinds of spices mixed, also a teacupful of black and one of white mustard seed, and two pounds of brown sugar; place a layer of the tomatoes in a porcelain kettle or a large tin utensil, then a layer of onions; over this a generous sprinkling of the mustard seed and spices; then sugar; repeat until your tomatoes and onions are used; pour over the best vinegar you can procure, and let it boil slowly half a day. This pickle will keep through cold and heat; nothing spoils it, if the vinegar is good.

Mrs. T. Ten Eyck,
Chicago, Ill.

SWEET CUCUMBER PICKLE—No. 1.

Take large green cucumbers, pare them and take

out the seeds with a silver spoon. Cut in large squares and boil in vinegar enough to cover until tender enough to pierce with a fork. Drain and put in a jar. To three pounds of cucumber make a syrup of one quart of vinegar, one pound of sugar, a few small pieces of cinnamon, a little mace, cloves and ginger root (tie the spices in a cloth). Heat the vinegar and spices and pour over the cucumbers. Repeat this five or six mornings. The last time put in glass jars and cover air tight.   Mrs. H. H. Brown,
Menomonie, Wis.

SWEET PICKLE PLUMS.

Five pounds of sugar, one pint of vinegar to seven pounds of plums, one tablespoonful of ground cinnamon, one teaspoonful of cloves and allspice. Boil all together until fruit is sufficiently cooked.

Mrs. A. Hoffman.

SWEET CUCUMBER PICKLE--No. 2.

Take cucumbers when fully ripe: pare them, cut lengthwise, and take out the seeds: put them into weak brine over night; in the morning, drain them. Boil tender in weak vinegar: drain again and put in jars. Turn over them a syrup (hot), made as follows: Allow to each pound of pickles, one-half pound of sugar, one-half cupful of vinegar; boil the vinegar and sugar a few minutes; add any spices you may like. Let boil, and skim well.   Mrs. B. Himmelsbach.

YELLOW PICKLE (Excellent).

Four quarts of sharp cider vinegar, four ounces of ground mustard (yellow), one ounce of white mustard, one ounce of bruised mace, one-half teaspoonful of ground cloves, one ounce of bruised ginger, three sticks of horseradish sliced, two ounces tumeric, tied in a bag, one teacupful of salt. The spices, without the tumeric, to be boiled in the vinegar a quarter of an hour. When cold, throw in the bag of tumeric. Make this pickle, and as vegetables come in season, throw them in, stirring from the bottom. It will keep for months. Use small string beans, onions, tiny ears of corn, beets, cauliflower, green tomatoes, cucumbers, etc.

Miss Grace Howe,

Kenosha, Wis.

Variety's the spice of life,
That gives it all its flavor.
—COWPER.

CATCHUPS AND SAUCES FOR MEATS, FISH AND VEGETABLES.

It is best to cook all sauces in a vessel set within a larger one of hot water, or use a "double boiler;" bottle and seal tomato catchup while hot, and it will not work ; be sure to boil it until the water has cooked well out of the tomatoes.

CAPER SAUCE (For Boiled Mutton).

One cupful of the liquor in which the meat has been boiled, two teaspoonfuls of flour rubbed smooth in a little water, salt to taste, two tablespoonfuls of butter, about two dozen capers or green nasturtium seeds ; heat the liquor to boiling and skim before stirring in the flour, which must be perfectly free from lumps, and rubbed smooth in cold water; stir until the sauce thickens evenly; when it has boiled a minute, add the butter, a little bit at a time, stirring constantly ; salt it and drop in the capers ; let it boil up once and turn in your sauce-boat.   J. W. SQUIRES.

CELERY SAUCE (For Boiled Turkey).

One pint best part of celery, cut very fine ; cook in boiling salted water until tender ; drain very dry ; add enough hot water to that in which the celery was cooked to make a pint; use this to make a good drawn butter into which put your cooked celery and seasoning.

CHILI SAUCE—No. 1.

Twenty-four large ripe tomatoes, six green peppers, four onions, three tablespoonfuls of salt, eight tablespoonfuls of brown sugar, six teacupfuls of vinegar; chop the peppers and onions very fine; peel the tomatoes and cut very small. Add one teaspoonful of cloves, one teaspoonful of allspice, and two teaspoonfuls of cinnamon. Put in a kettle and boil gently an hour.

CHILI SAUCE—No. 2.

Eighteen large ripe cucumbers, one onion, two small red peppers; chop fine; mix and add four cupfuls of vinegar, two tablespoonfuls of salt, two teaspoonfuls of ginger, four tablespoonfuls of sugar, two teaspoonfuls each of cinnamon, cloves and allspice, one teaspoonful of nutmeg.　　　　Miss Wilson,

Menomonie, Wis.

CUCUMBER CATCHUP.

Twelve large green cucumbers and three onions, grated fine; press the pulp as dry as possible in a thin cloth; add pepper and salt to taste; pour on vinegar until as thick as horseradish prepared for table use. Seal tight. This catchup, brought out on a winter's day, will prove very appetizing, and perfume the room like fresh cucumbers.

Mrs. H. O. Crane,

Green Bay, Wis.

DRAWN BUTTER (For Fish, Cabbage or Cauliflower).

One heaping tablespoonful of butter rubbed into two heaping teaspoonfuls of flour. Set in a pan of hot water; keep stirring, and when it warms, season with salt and pepper, and pour over it slowly a teacupful of boiling water. Mix with milk for puddings, and water for vegetables, fish or meats. Boil one minute. To make this richer, pour it boiling hot into the yolks of two well-beaten eggs. Just before serving, stir and serve it at once.   Mrs. G. C. Ginty.

HORSERADISH SAUCE (Hot for Beef).

Four tablespoonfuls of grated horseradish, four of powdered cracker, one-half cupful of cream, one teaspoonful of powdered sugar, a little salt, one-half saltspoonful of pepper, one even teaspoonful of made mustard, two tablespoonfuls of vinegar. Mix all together and heat in a vessel over hot water.   Marion Harland.

HOLLANDAISE SAUCE (For Baked or Boiled Fish).

One-half cupful of butter, yolks of two eggs, juice of half a lemon, one-half cupful of boiling water, saltspoonful of salt, one-quarter saltspoonful of cayenne pepper. Rub the butter to a cream; add the yolks one at a time and beat well; then the lemon juice, salt and pepper. Just before serving, add the boiling water and stir rapidly until it thickens like custard. Pour the sauce around the fish.   Mrs. Parloa.

MAÎTRE DÉ HOTEL BUTTER (For Beefsteak).

One quarter cup of butter, one-half teaspoonful of salt, one-half of pepper, one tablespoonful of chopped parsley, one of lemon juice; rub the butter to a cream; add the other ingredients and spread on hot beafsteak. You may add a little onion juice if you like.

COOKING SCHOOL.

MINT SAUCE.

One cupful of fresh chopped mint, one-quarter cupful of sugar, one-half cupful of vinegar; use only the leaves and tender tips of the mint; let it stand an hour before serving. This is very nice with roast lamb.

COOKING SCHOOL.

MUSHROOM SAUCE—No. 1.

Half a canful of mushrooms, boiled and chopped, a cupful of good meat gravy strained over them; stew five minutes; thicken with browned flour and season well.   M. N.

MUSHROOM SAUCE—No. 2.

One canful of mushrooms, chopped fine, one pint of cream, butter the size of an egg, salt, pepper and lemon juice; thicken with browned flour and cook until thick.   MRS. A. J. McGILVRAY.

RAW TOMATO CATCHUP.

One-half peck of ripe tomatoes, skinned and chopped fine, two roots of horseradish grated, one teacupful of salt, one teacupful of black and white mustard seed mixed, two tablespoonfuls of black pepper, two red peppers, chopped fine, three stalks of celery, and one cupful of onions chopped fine, one teaspoonful each of powdered cloves, mace and cinnamon, one cupful of brown sugar, one quart of vinegar. Fit for use immediately.

MISS HATTIE WHITNEY,

Green Bay, Wis.

SPICED CURRANTS (To be eaten with Meats).

Eleven pounds of currants, one pint of vinegar, eight pounds of sugar, nine teaspoonfuls of cinnamon, six of cloves, four of allspice, one of mace, one small nutmeg. Boil until thick, and put into glasses like jelly.

TOMATO CATCHUP—No. 1.

To one gallon of cooked tomato juice and pulp, after it has been put through a sieve, add four tablespoonfuls of salt, two of black pepper, one of chopped green peppers, three of cinnamon, two of ground mustard, and one of cloves, one quart of vinegar. Boil until thick, and bottle at once.   MRS. A. HOFFMAN.

TOMATO CATCHUP—No. 2.

Cook one-half bushel of tomatoes thoroughly, rub through a sieve and boil to a jelly. To each gallon of the jelly add one pint of vinegar (scant), four table-spoonfuls of salt, four of black pepper, four of cinnamon, three of cloves, one-half teaspoonful of cayenne pepper, one-quarter cupful of mustard. Boil one hour. Bottle while hot, and seal with beeswax, rosin, etc.

MRS. C. P. BARKER.

TOMATO SAUCE.

One-half can tomatoes, one cupful of water, two allspice berries, two pepper corns, two cloves, a sprig of parsley, one tablespoonful of chopped onion, one of butter, one heaping tablespoonful of corn starch. Salt and pepper to taste. Put the tomatoes, water, spices and parsley on to boil in a granite sauce-pan; fry the onions in the butter until yellow; add the corn starch, and stir all into the tomato; simmer ten minutes; add salt, pepper and a little cayenne. Strain sauce over boiled meat or fish.

WHITE SAUCE (For Croquettes, Meat or Fish).

One pint of hot cream, two even tablespoonfuls of butter, four heaping tablespoonfuls of flour; season to taste with salt, pepper and a few grains of cayenne; add one-quarter teaspoonful of celery salt. Scald the cream; melt the butter, and add to it the dry flour; mix well; add part of the cream and stir until it thickens; add more cream, and when boiling and perfectly smooth add the rest of the cream (the sauce should be very thick, almost like a drop batter). Add the seasoning, and mix while hot with meat or fish. If this sauce is used for croquettes, a beaten egg may be added to it. Milk may be used instead of cream by adding more butter.   COOKING SCHOOL.

SALADS AND SALAD DRESSINGS.

Salads are a religion. Time, which destroys creeds, rounds and mellows into ripe completeness the art of compounding this dish for the gods. The ability of skillfully and artistically concocting a salad argues a mental perfection beside which all mere moral excellence sinks into insignificance. To mix a salad is a solemn rite; a ceremony only to be undertaken with deliberation, gravity and reverence. He who has once made a good salad, neither cutting nor bruising the herbs—who has been betrayed into no mixture therewith of fish, flesh or fowl, degrading the whole to the vulgar level of a mongrel mayonnaise—who has added exactly the proper dash of white wine, and served it cool, piquant, green, fragrant, crackling, appealing to all five senses at once, has achieved the triumph of being and has nobly vindicated his claim to existence.

—Arlo Bates.

SALADS.

A salad to be good must be *cold* when served. When oil is used, the dressing requires a great deal of mixing or blending. When the boiled dressings are used, have them perfectly *smooth*, which can be done by constant stirring when on the fire; *do not add the eggs when the other ingredients are on the verge of boiling*, but stir them in when the mixture is *warm* and keep stirring until they come to a boiling heat, when the dressing will be thick enough to remove from the fire. When lettuce is used, wash it in ice water, *break* it apart and drain it on a fine sieve, or stretch a piece of cheese cloth over something handy, and drain it on that, taking care to keep it cool.

The salad receipts given here will give perfect satisfaction if made according to rule. They have been served to hundreds of people by the ladies who gave them to this book, and have virtually paid off debts, helped build a parsonage, and been the very root and foundation of many good works.

CHICKEN SALAD—No. 1. (Enough for a Party.)

Take as much celery as chicken; pick the chicken up in small pieces; cut the celery about as large as a white bean; set on the ice until you need it; then mix together and salt and pepper it. Pour over the following dressing which has been made long enough to be perfectly cold: Yolks of eight eggs, one cupful of butter, two cupfuls of vinegar, one-fourth of a cupful of sugar, one tablespoonful of made mustard, one teaspoonful of salt, one of black pepper, and a pinch of red pepper, one large cupful of sweet cream. (Half this receipt will do for family use.) Put your vinegar, butter, salt, pepper and sugar on the stove to heat; when *warm* stir in the yolks of the eggs which have been previously well beaten; stir until the mixture boils or thickens to the consistency of custard; set away to cool, and when perfectly cool add the mustard and cream. You can use more cream.

CHICKEN SALAD—No. 2.

One quart of chicken, shredded as fine as you like; season to taste with salt and pepper; one quart of celery cut in small pieces, three or four hard boiled eggs sliced very fine; mix lightly together, and put where it will keep cold until time for serving. Then mix with it the following dressing, and garnish with parsley, delicate celery leaves, slices of hard boiled eggs, or lemons sliced very thin:

Dressing.—Yolks of four eggs, three tablespoonfuls of sugar, one teaspoonful of salt, one-half teaspoonful of pepper, one teaspoonful of ground mustard, four tablespoonfuls of vinegar; mix together and heat in a basin set in a kettle of boiling water; stir constantly until it thickens; remove from the fire; stir into it one tablespoonful of butter, and five tablespoonfuls of lemon juice. When cold, thin this dressing with sweet cream to a proper consistency, and mix with the chicken.   Mrs. A. HOFFMAN.

CHICKEN SALAD—No. 3.

Equal parts of chicken and celery, cut into small pieces with a knife (string the celery before using). Make the following dressing and mix with it:

Dressing.—One-half cupful of vinegar, one-half teaspoonful of dry mustard, a pinch of cayenne, one tablespoonful of butter, one of sugar, a teaspoonful of salt; mix all together and heat; when warm, add two well beaten eggs; stir them in slowly, and when thick, put away to cool. When cold, add one-half cupful of whipped cream and the juice of one or two lemons. If you do not use it at once, do not add the cream and lemon until you serve the salad.   Mrs. C. E. TOBY,
                                        Eau Claire, Wis.

CABBAGE SALAD—No. 1.

Slice the cabbage fine, and for one small head make the following dressing: Yolks of three eggs, three tablespoonfuls of sugar, one teaspoonful of salt, one-half teaspoonful of pepper, one teaspoonful of ground mustard, eight tablespoonfuls of vinegar; beat all together. Put in a basin; set in a kettle of boiling water; stir constantly until it thickens; remove from fire; add a heaping tablespoonful of butter, and when cold, thin with sweet cream, and pour over and mix with the cabbage.   Mrs. G. Tabor Thompson,

Eau Claire, Wis.

CABBAGE SALAD—No. 2.

Chop your cabbage. Make a dressing as follows: One-half cupful of vinegar, a small piece of butter, one egg, two teaspoonfuls of sugar, four teaspoonfuls of milk, a little salt; set the vinegar on to boil, and when boiling, stir in the other ingredients. When thick, pour over the cabbage.   Mrs. Will Talmadge.

CELERY SALAD.

Cut your celery into bits half an inch long and set on ice while you prepare your dressing. Take four hard boiled eggs (yolks only), one raw egg well beaten, one teaspoonful of salt, one-half saltspoonful of cayenne pepper, one teaspoonful of white sugar, one tablespoonful of salad oil, two teaspoonfuls of made mustard, one small teacupful of vinegar. Rub the yolks of the eggs to a smooth paste, adding by degrees the salt, pepper, sugar, mustard and oil. Beat the raw egg to a froth and stir it in; add the vinegar. This dressing must be cold when you pour it over the celery. If hot weather when you make it, stir a lump of ice in it for a few minutes; remove and pour at once over your salad.

CUCUMBER SALAD.

Place crisp lettuce heads in the bottom of a salad dish, next a thick layer of sliced cucumbers (have the cucumbers in ice water some time before you need them), over this a layer of ripe tomatoes cut very thin. Pour over all a French or Mayonnaise dressing and set on ice until it is served. This is a nice relish when you serve a dinner in courses.

GERMAN SALAD.

Chop up six boiled potatoes, two red beets (boiled), one raw onion, two heads of celery, two apples, a small piece of salt salmon or herring. Dress with vinegar, pepper, oil and mustard ; garnish your dish with lettuce leaves.   MRS. HIMMELSBACH.

LOBSTER SALAD.

Half as much celery as lobster, cut in squares about the size of a bean. Save out the red claws or coral part to garnish your dish. When you take your lobster from the can, drain it as dry as possible before using; add the whites of four hard boiled eggs, chopped, and put the yolks through the ricer to garnish the top after the salad is all ready to serve. This receipt refers to canned lobster, as we cannot obtain the fresh in our home market. Use salad dressing No. 1 (boiled) to mix with.   MRS. GEO. C. GINTY.

MEDLEY SALAD.

One cupful of salmon cut in squares, one-half cupful of lobster cut the same, three hard boiled eggs : slice the whites of the eggs into the salmon and lobster, add one cupful of finely cut celery and one cupful of shredded lettuce ; put the yolks of the eggs through the ricer to garnish the top. Use any of the dressings you may choose.

POTATO SALAD—No. 1.

Take cold boiled potatoes, hard boiled eggs and a raw onion ; pack in a dish a layer of the potatoes sliced thin, next the onion chipped fine, then the eggs sliced. Pour over each layer a little of the following dressing : Salad oil one-half a gill, vinegar one-half a gill, one teaspoonful of mustard, one-half a teaspoonful of pepper, one of salt. Boil eight eggs for an ordinary salad.

MRS. L. B. CRUTTENDEN.

POTATO SALAD No. 2.

Eight boiled potatoes cut in small squares, one onion cut fine, six hard boiled eggs cut in small bits; add a little celery, if you like ; use French or boiled dressing, or take the yolks of four hard boiled eggs and blend them smooth with a half cupful of melted butter, a teaspoonful of made mustard, a little salt and pepper, a little vinegar, and cream to thin it to the proper consistency.

SALMON SALAD.

One can of fresh salmon, two large heads of lettuce. Drain all the oil from the salmon and shred it up in small pieces. Pick the lettuce up, and with a fork mix the fish with it, adding three hard boiled eggs which have been chopped. Pour over it a dressing made as follows :

Yolks of two eggs well beaten, a little salt and pepper to taste, one teaspoonful of sugar, two of made mustard, one tablespoonful of butter, a pinch of red pepper; stir into this mixture three tablespoonfuls of vinegar; set in a kettle of hot water and stir until it thickens. When perfectly cold, thin with cream and pour over the salmon and lettuce. Place rings of hard boiled egg over the top, and serve.

Fish salads are pretty served in nests of lettuce leaves or in shells, which you can buy at the crockery stores. MRS. GEO. C. GINTY.

SHRIMP SALAD.

Wash the shrimps in cold water thoroughly, break up with a fork into small bits; cut into squares four medium-sized cucumber pickles; chop fine the whites of two hard boiled eggs, cream the yolks with melted butter the size of a large egg; mix with the shrimps, pickles, eggs and whites of eggs. Make as wet as you desire with the following dressing: One cupful of vinegar, a tablespoonful of mustard, teaspoonful of salt, a little pepper, butter the size of a large egg, two eggs; heat the vinegar and other ingredients, and when warm, add the beaten eggs ; stir gently until it thickens. Many like it without the first dressing.

MRS. T. J. CUNNINGHAM.

TOMATO SALAD.

Make a thick bed of crisp lettuce leaves on a good-sized platter; cut nice, large, red tomatoes in thick slices; pepper, salt and lay on top of the lettuce; place on the ice. Just before serving, pour over the top either French or mayonnaise dressing, or the dressing used in chicken salad No. 1. When you serve, cut down through the lettuce and have some of it and a good slice of the tomato on each plate. This is a pretty looking salad and is nice for a dinner course. Do not have your dressing thin.   Mrs. Geo. C. Ginty.

SALAD DRESSINGS.

BOILED DRESSING—No. 1.

Yolks of eight eggs, a cupful of butter, two of vinegar, quarter cupful of sugar, one teaspoonful of salt, one of black pepper, one tablespoonful of made mustard, a pinch of red pepper, one large cupful of cream. (Half this receipt will do for ordinary occasions.) Beat the yolks of the eggs very light; place the other ingredients (except the cream and mustard) on the stove to heat; when warm, add the eggs, stirring constantly until it comes to a boil, when it will be a smooth, thick custard. When cold, add the mustard and cream.

BOILED DRESSING—No. 2.

Yolks of three eggs well beaten, one teaspoonful of mustard, two teaspoonfuls of salt, one-fourth saltspoonful of cayenne, two tablespoonfuls of sugar, two table-

spoonfuls of melted butter or oil, one cupful of cream
or milk, half-cupful of hot vinegar, whites of three
eggs beaten stiff; cook in the double boiler until it
thickens like soft custard ; stir well. If you keep it in
a cool place it will be good for two weeks. This is nice
for boiled cabbage, cauliflower, etc.

Mrs. Walrath,
Cooking School.

BOILED DRESSING—No. 3. (For Cold Slaw.)

Boil half a cupful of vinegar with two teaspoonfuls
of sugar; add a little salt, pepper and mustard, if you
like ; rub a quarter of a cupful of butter to a cream,
with one heaping teaspoonful of flour, and pour the
boiling vinegar on it. Cook four or five minutes,
and then pour the entire mixture over a well-beaten
egg (the yolk only); turn this over one good pint of
red or white chopped cabbage, and set away to cool.

FRENCH DRESSING.

Three tablespoonfuls of olive oil, saltspoonful of salt,
half a one of pepper, one-quarter teaspoonful of onion
juice, one tablespoonful of vinegar; add the oil last,
stirring constantly, and a little of it at a time. You
can take lemon juice instead of the vinegar and add a
teaspoonful of made mustard if you like.

MAYONNAISE DRESSING.

One teaspoonful of mustard, one of powdered sugar,
one-half saltspoonful of salt, a pinch of cayenne pepper,
yolks of two raw eggs, one pint of olive oil, two tablespoonfuls of vinegar, two of lemon juice; mix the first

four ingredients in a small bowl; add the eggs; stir well; add the oil, a few drops at a time, stirring constantly with a fork until it thickens. Do not try to stir it all in at once, but very gradually. When the dressing becomes thick, thin it with a little lemon; then add more oil and lemon alternately, and lastly add the vinegar. Should the egg not thicken quickly, one-half teaspoonful of the unbeaten white of an egg or a few drops of vinegar will often have the desired effect, and also keep it smooth. Just before you use it, add one-half cupful of whipped cream. Never mix the mayonnaise dressing with the meat or fish until ready to serve, and then leave half of it to pour over the top.

SALAD DRESSING THAT WILL KEEP.

One scant half cupful of mustard; one tablespoonful of sugar; mix together with a little hot water; beat the yolks of eighteen eggs with a pinch of red pepper, and five teaspoonfuls of salt; add the mustard, eight tablespoonfuls of olive oil, one and one-half cupfuls of butter, melted, one and one-half cupfuls of vinegar, juice of two small lemons. Make in an earthen dish and stir constantly lest it separate; put in a glass jar with a screw top. When you use, add one quart of whipped cream. The above is enough dressing for four large year-old chickens.

Miss Hattie Whitney,

Green Bay, Wis.

SALMON SALAD DRESSING.

Yolks of two eggs, well beaten, a teaspoonful of salt and black pepper each, two teaspoonfuls of white sugar, two teaspoonfuls of made mustard, one table-spoonful of butter. Stir into this mixture four table-spoonfuls of best vinegar. Put the dressing into a bowl and set in a kettle of hot water; stir until it thickens; when cold, thin with cream.

Mrs. Will Talmadge.

"For I, who hold Sage Homer's rule the best,
Welcome the coming, speed the parting guest."

RELISHES AND HINTS FOR THE TABLE.

CHEESE STICKS.

These are used as a relish. Roll puff paste thin; sprinkle with grated cheese; fold, roll out and sprinkle again; repeat this several times. Place on the ice to harden. When cold, roll into rectangular shape, one-eighth of an inch thick. Place on a dripper, bottom side up, and with a knife dipped in hot water, cut into strips four or five inches long, and less than a quarter of an inch wide. Bake and serve piled cob-house fashion. These are nice for a lunch party.

SALTED ALMONDS.

Blanch the almonds; have ready a pan of fine hot salt, and, while wet, drop the nuts in the hot salt. Take them out and place in a dripper, with a paper on the bottom. Set in the oven and brown; watch them closely, and take from the oven as fast as they turn a light brown. Use for a relish, as you would olives.

Mrs. B. E. Reid.

Hard boiled eggs put through a ricer make a pretty garnish for salads, fish, etc. Shake gently over the top as they come from the ricer.

A PRETTY WAY TO SERVE FRIED OYSTERS.

Bake a square loaf of bread, a little longer than usual, so as to have a good brown crust; stand on end and cut off the top; take the inside all out; fill up with fried oysters. Stand it on a pretty plate, tie a bright ribbon around the center; put the top on to keep them warm, and set the loaf on the table before the hostess who will serve them from the loaf, with a silver oyster fork. Very nice for a lunch party.

TO SERVE OLIVES.

Olives are much more appetizing served in little dishes of pounded ice.

In serving an "Orange Charlotte" or a mold of Blanc Mange, make two or three orange baskets; fill them with different colored jellies, and garnish the dish with them, by putting one at each end and on either side of the mold or form. Tie a bright ribbon on the handles of the baskets. To make the orange basket, you cut away half the orange, leaving a strip of the skin about half an inch wide for the handle. Remove the pulp from the other half orange, and the strip of skin across the top and you have the basket. Pink it around with the scissors, and tie a bright ribbon on the handle. You can make orange jelly of the pulp if you use many of the oranges at one time.

MOCK ORANGES.

Cut off the ends of oranges, remove the pulp without breaking the skin, fill the skins with Charlotte Russe or wine or lemon jelly; set in a pan of ice until time to serve.

CHARLOTTE RUSSE.

To serve Charlotte Russe—Buy little fancy baskets at the confectioner's or line old-fashioned tumblers with lady-fingers; fill half full of Charlotte Russe and when cold, turn out. Place the forms on pretty little plates and serve with cake.

OYSTERS. TURBOT OR FISH SALADS.

To serve scolloped oysters, turbot or fish salads—Use oyster shells nicely cleaned, or shells that you can buy for the purpose at any large store where such things are sold.

In the summer season, fish salads are very pretty served in nests of lettuce leaves. You can make the nests very readily by using what is known as "head lettuce."

A bouquet should always brighten the table in summer, and if you can afford it, in the winter season as well.

Serve Saratoga chips in fancy paper baskets, which you can make or buy.

TO CHRYSTALLIZE FRUIT.

Pour a cupful of boiling water over a cupful of granulated sugar, and let the mixture boil slowly, without stirring, one-half hour. Dip a skewer into the syrup and then in cold water. If the thread formed break off brittle, the syrup is ready. Keep your syrup in a bowl set in a pan of hot water, while you are using it. Cherries, English walnuts, currants and sections of orange are pretty prepared in this way for table ornamentation.

CHEESE CRACKERS.

Take large round milk crackers, butter them; put them on a buttered paper in a dripper; put on each grated cheese about an inch thick, and a teaspoonful of cream. Set in a slow oven. Let them remain until the cracker consumes the cheese, and they are a light brown. Nice to serve with lettuce for lunch.

MRS. WM. O'NEIL.

A pretty way to send oranges to the table is to cut the rind from the ends and leave a strip round the middle, then open, leaving the sections on the strip of peel.

CHANTILLY BASKETS.

Dip the edges of soft flexible macaroons in syrup prepared as for crystallized fruit and make little baskets; fill with candy, jelly, fruit, etc. Use for ornamenting your table.

Serve raw oysters in a cake of ice; cut with a chissel and hammer a pretty block, and with a hot flat-ron, melt a place in the center; lay the oysters in; set the block of ice on a platter and send to the table.

TO GARNISH WITH COLORED EGGS.

To garnish a dish of molded jelly, a form of Charlotte Russe or Russian cream, turn the form out on a fancy platter or in a pretty dish, lay around it eggs made of gelatine Blanc Mange and colored. To make the eggs: Break a hole in the end of an egg and let the contents of the shell run out as thoroughly as possible; rinse out the shell with cold water, and as fast as you get them ready, set in a pan of bran or cornmeal; make your Blanc Mange and dip out portions of it into bowls, leaving some for white eggs; stir a little grape jelly into one of the bowls and you have the material for blue eggs; in another chocolate and you have brown eggs; in another cochineal (a few drops) and you have pink eggs. Fill up the empty shells with these mixtures and set away to cool. When cold, peel the shells off, rinse the Blanc Mange eggs in very cold water and use to garnish your dish. It is better to make the eggs the day before you want to use them.

Nasturtium blossoms make a beautiful garnish for a dish, and as they are edible it makes no difference if one drops into the salad or whatever you are serving.

Horseradish is very nice mixed with cream and vinegar. Mix slowly.

MEMORANDA.

MEMORANDA.

MEMORANDA.

SOUPS.

If you thicken a soup with flour or corn starch,
always let it boil five or ten minutes after the thickening is in, to prevent the *raw taste*, which spoils a soup.

If you cannot get all the fat from the stock after it
has jellied, wring a cloth out of hot water and wipe the
top of the stock.

If you put dumplings in a soup or on top of a stew,
draw the soup or stew to the back of the stove, and, after
you have covered the dumplings, leave them to cook
and the soup or stew to simmer for twenty minutes
before you raise the cover. Thickened soups should
be the consistency of good cream.

You can buy bay leaves and herbs that the soups
require at drug stores.

AMBER SOUP.

Four pounds of shin beef, four pounds of knuckle
of veal, or three pounds of fowl, four quarts of cold
water, two ounces of lean ham or bacon, six whole cloves,
six whole pepper corns, one tablespoonful of herbs, one
tablespoonful of salt, three small onions, one carrot, one
turnip, two stalks of celery, two sprigs of parsley, one saltspoonful of celery seed. To clarify: Rind of one lemon,
whites and shells of three eggs.

BOUILLON—No. 1.

Four pounds of beef, two pounds of bone, two quarts of cold water, one tablespoonful of salt, four pepper corns, four cloves, one tablespoonful of herbs; let boil until reduced to three pints. Set away in an earthen jar.

BOUILLON—No. 2.

Four pounds of beef from the middle of the round, two pounds of bone, two quarts of cold water, one table-spoonful of salt, a few pepper corns, three cloves, a little parsley; wipe the meat and bones; cut into small pieces; add the water and heat slowly; add the season-ing, and simmer four or five hours. Boil it down to three pints; set it away to cool; remove the fat from the top: heat again, and add salt and pepper. Serve for lunch, or use for sick people needing strength.

Mrs. J. W. Squires.

BEAN SOUP.

One cupful of beans; parboil in soda water; pour off water as soon as it boils, and add two quarts of cold water; salt, pepper and butter to taste. Let cook slowly three or four hours. Instead of butter, salt pork may be added. Pea soup may be made in the same manner as the bean soup.

BEEF SOUP.

To a joint bone of beef add cold water, one quart to a pound; boil slowly, and skim often. Boil three hours. Add one-half cupful of rice, one good-sized potato, one small onion; chop one-half cupful of meat, and add with the vegetables.

Boil two hours. Dry celery left from the table, and keep for seasoning soups. Mrs. A. Hoffman.

CREAM OF CELERY SOUP.

The flesh of the chicken from which the stock is to be made should, with the exception of the breast, with the skin perfect as possible, be placed in the pot and removed as soon as tender. To each quart of stock, when strained and skimmed, add one ounce of rice, and let simmer three-fourths of an hour; then add the breast of the chicken finely shredded, and a pint of cream thickened with flour; season to taste with pepper and salt; let boil two minutes: flavor with celery, and serve.

CORN SOUP--No. 1.

One pint of grated green corn, one quart of milk, one pint of hot water, one heaping tablespoonful of butter, one slice of onion. Cook the corn in the water thirty minutes. Let the milk and onions come to a boil. Have the flour and butter mixed together, and add a few tablespoonfuls of the boiling milk. When perfectly smooth, stir in the milk, and cook eight minutes. Take out the onion, and add the corn; season to taste, and serve.

CORN SOUP—No. 2.

One can of corn cooked one hour; then strain. Put one quart of milk on stove, season with butter, pepper, salt and a little celery salt. When the milk boils, put in soup dish with the strained corn. Have ready two eggs well beaten and stir in lightly.

NELLIE BRIGGS,

Milwaukee, Wis.

CHICKEN SOUP.

Save the broth after boiling chickens, and to it add two onions thinly sliced; boil twenty minutes; season with salt and pepper; add two beaten eggs, and serve.

ENGLISH RECEIPT.

DUMPLINGS FOR SOUP—No. 1.

Make the same dough you would for "Baking Powder Biscuit," with less shortening. Cut out with biscuit cutter. Cover and cook twenty minutes.

MRS. R. F. WILSON,

Eau Claire, Wis.

DUMPLINGS FOR SOUP—No. 2.

One pint of flour, one teaspoonful of baking powder, one egg, butter size of a butternut, a little salt, milk enough to mix a stiff batter which will drop from a spoon. Boil twenty minutes.

GREEN PEA SOUP—No. 1.

Cover a can of green peas with hot water and boil with an onion until they will mash easily. The time will depend on the age of the peas, say from twenty to thirty minutes. Mash and add a pint of soup stock; cook together with two tablespoonfuls of butter and one of flour until smooth, but not brown; add these to the peas with one cupful of milk and one of cream. Season with salt and pepper and let it boil up once : add a cup of whipped cream before serving, if you have it. Three cupfuls of milk may be used instead of cream. Squares of bread to serve with above : Cut the bread in little squares and fry in hot lard until just browned. A little salt may be used if desired.   Mrs. R. B. Clarke.

GREEN PEA SOUP—No. 2.

One can of green peas warmed and rubbed through a purée strainer; when nearly all rubbed through, pour one pint of hot milk through the strainer, to rinse off every part of the pulp. Put the pulp and milk on to boil, add more milk and cream if you have it, until you have the proper consistency, which will be about like cream; when boiling, thicken with one table-spoonful of butter, one-half tablespoonful of salt, one scant teaspoonful of sugar and a dash of white pepper. Serve with buttered crackers which have been browned in the oven.

MUTTON BROTH.

Allow a quart of water to each pound of meat and bone; break the bones and cut the meat into small pieces; cover with cold water, and heat slowly; add salt, pepper and a little turnip (and onion, if you like it); simmer until the meat is in shreds. Strain it, and when cool, take off the fat. To one quart of the broth, allow two tablespoonfuls of rice, washed and soaked half an hour. When the broth is boiling, add the rice. Simmer until the rice is cooked, and serve at once, while hot.   English.

NOODLES FOR SOUP--No. 1.

To one beaten egg, add as much flour as it will absorb, a little salt, and roll them as a wafer. Leave to dry three hours. Dust lightly with flour; roll over into a large roll, slice thin from the ends. Shake out loosely : put in the boiling soup, and boil rapidly ten minutes.   MRS. WM. SQUIRES.

NOODLES FOR SOUP--No. 2.

For every egg, one tablespoonful of milk, and a little salt; work all the flour into it that you possibly can; roll out; spread with flour; roll "over and over," and cut down in rings.   MRS. R. F. WILSON,

Eau Claire, Wis.

OYSTER SOUP.

One quart of oysters, one ditto sweet milk, one-fourth pound of butter. Set the milk on the stove, and let it come to a boil. After the oysters are cooked, add two tablespoonfuls of grated cracker; pepper and salt to taste. It is better if you use cream instead of the milk.   MRS. L. H. CUSHING.

ONE DAY SOUP.

Half a can of tomatoes, five or six cold boiled or baked potatoes, half an onion, one stalk of celery, or a few celery tops. Boil all together until the vegetables are very soft. Put through a colander, add pepper and salt, and a pinch of sugar. Just before serving, pour in one cup of hot milk with a pinch of soda dissolved in it; sift over the top a few very dry bread crumbs.

ENGLISH COOK BOOK.

PEA SOUP—No. 1.

Two cupfuls of peas soaked over night in cold water; put into three quarts of cold water and set on the stove to boil; add one small bay leaf, four onions cut fine, and fried in one-half a cupful of butter; salt and pepper to taste, and let it boil until well done. A little celery may be added if desired.

Mrs. A. B. LaRocque.

PEA SOUP—No. 2.

Boil a piece of the shank of beef until it is tender; have ready one pint of split peas which have been thoroughly cooked, mashed and put through a colander; add them to the soup with two onions, sliced, one-half a teaspoonful of celery seed; salt and pepper to taste. Boil all together for three-fourths of an hour.

PEA SOUP (Split Peas).

Four pounds of meat, one of split peas, four quarts of water. Boil together three or four hours adding more water if necessary. Season and strain for the table.

STOCK FOR SOUP—No. 1.

Take fresh, juicy, lean meat (bones and meat of about equal weight), put into cold water in the proportion of two half pints to each pound, salt slightly and set on the stove; do not allow to boil for the first half hour: simmer slowly, partly covered for four or five hours. Season at the last moment; when the soup is cold, remove the fat: the stock underneath will form a jelly, and in cool weather will keep a week.

Chicken or turkey bones will add to the delicacy of the soup. Good soup can also be made by using the trimmings of fresh meat, bits of cold cooked beef, or the bones of any meat or fowl. Just before dinner each day, it is only necessary to cut off some of the jelly and heat it; it is very good with nothing additional, but one can have a change, by adding different flavorings, such as macaroni, vermicelli, tomatoes, or some other vegetable.

STOCK FOR SOUP—No. 2.

Three pounds of thin rib beef, one-half pound of liver; put on to cook with cold water. Let it come to a boiling point and skim very thoroughly; add salt; let it boil up gently, and skim again. Add one carrot, one turnip, a small piece of cabbage, one large onion (stick into it three or four cloves), one small bay leaf. Boil slowly until the meat is well done. Strain and put away for use. Any kind of soup can be made from this stock.   Mrs. A. B. LaRocque.

SOUP STOCK (Brown).—No. 3.

Six pounds hind shin of beef, six quarts of cold water, ten whole cloves, ten whole pepper corns, a bouquet of herbs, one large tablespoonful of salt, three small onions, one carrot, one turnip, two stalks of celery, two sprigs of parsley. Wipe, and cut the meat and bones into small pieces. Put the marrow bones, half the meat and the cold water into the kettle. Soak half an hour before heating; add the herbs and spices; brown the onions and the remainder of the meat, and add them to the stock : then the vegetables chopped fine. Simmer six or seven hours, and strain. This stock is good in tomato soup, or any kind you choose to use it for.

OLD HOUSEKEEPER.

SOUP A LA JULIENNE.

Three tablespoonfuls of butter, three slices of salt pork cut in small squares. Put these ingredients in a kettle with two tablespoonfuls of nicely browned flour (be careful not to burn the flour in browning); add three quarts of boiling water, two carrots, four potatoes, a large turnip, a small piece of cabbage and two onions—all chopped or cut fine. Season with a little celery, parsley, a bay leaf, salt, black pepper, a pinch of cayenne and a small piece of garlic. Cook all together for two hours and a half with a slow fire. Any kind of meat broth or gravey may be added if desired, but it is good without. Mrs. A. B. LaRocque.

TURKEY SOUP.

Take the carcase of the turkey, leaving what dressing adheres to the bones, add three quarts of water and boil down to two; then strain carefully, leaving the soup to cool over night. When cool skim off the fat. While warming add one teaspoonful of cinnamon, one-half ditto of cloves and allspice, one-quarter ditto mace, and sufficient browned flour to thicken a little. Just before serving add a sliced lemon and a hard boiled egg cut into small pieces. OLD HOUSEKEEPER.

TURTLE SOUP.

Turn the turtle on his back, cut off the head so that the blood will all run out. Let it remain over night. Lay it on its back again, open it on the sides, take all the meat and eggs out and let them lay in water twenty-four hours. To make the soup: Boil the turtle meat in salt and water; when about half cooked take out and put away to cool. Add to the broth two slices of salt pork cut in small pieces, two tablespoonfuls of flour, two of butter (browned nicely), one small bay leaf, three cloves, one onion (cut fine), a little pepper, nutmeg and parsley, the yolks of six hard boiled eggs (whole), a little lemon juice, cayenne, black pepper and salt. Cut the turtle meat in small squares and put in the broth again, boil until well done. Five minutes before serving add one can of mushrooms and a glass of sherry wine. Calf's head may be used in place of the turtle.   MRS. A. B. LaRocque.

TOMATO SOUP—No. 1.

One can of tomatoes cooked half an hour with a teaspoonful of sugar and soda the size of a pea. Put this through a fine sieve and add one pint of soup stock, which has been strained. Stick three or four cloves into half a large onion; brown this in two tablespoonfuls of butter; add this to the soup and boil one hour. Skim out the onion and cloves. Thicken with a tablespoonful of flour; boil five minutes or more after the thickening is in the soup. Put diamonds or little squares of buttered bread browned in the oven, in the bottom of your soup-tureen with a cupful of whipped cream; pour the soup over and serve.

                    MRS. WM. O'NEIL.

TOMATO SOUP—No. 2.

Cut two carrots, two onions and three ounces of salt pork into small pieces; add a sprig of parsley and fry slowly for fifteen minutes in three ounces of butter. Put in three tablespoonfuls of flour; mix well; add this to two cans of tomatoes and two quarts of veal broth; season with salt and pepper. Cook slowly for one hour. Pass through a sieve; boil again; add two ounces of butter, a little fine sugar, and serve with small squares of bread fried in butter.

Mrs. A. J. McGilvray.

TOMATO SOUP—No. 3.

One can of tomatoes, one and one-half quarts of milk, one small teaspoonful of soda, flour to thicken, butter, pepper and salt to taste; put the milk on the stove and when boiling, thicken; at the same time have the tomatoes cooking with a little water added to them; season them, add a little butter and just before serving add a very small teaspoonful of soda to the tomatoes; pour quickly into the milk and strain while it is effer- vescing. Mrs. Frank Rotch,

Bucoda, Wash. T.

TOMATO SOUP—No. 4

Cook tomatoes in usual manner; when well cooked, add one-half teaspoonful of soda; stir well; then pour in one quart of new milk and let boil. Season same as oyster soup. J. R. Congdon.

TOMATO SOUP—No. 5.

One quart of tomatoes, one quart of milk, heated in

separate dishes; when tomatoes come to a boil, add one-half a teaspoonful of soda and stir well; skim and strain.   Season with butter, pepper and salt to taste; when ready to serve, add the heated milk to tomatoes.

Mrs. A. Hoffman.

FRESH FISH, SALT FISH, OYSTERS, ETC.

After cleaning a fish be sure to wipe it dry, particularly if you intend to broil it. Broil on a greased wire broiler over clear coals, the fleshy side first, as the skin side burns easily. In soaking salt fish, soak in sour milk, *skin side* up, so that the salt may soak away from the fish. In baking a fish use as little moisture as possible and the fish will be dry and flake off in nice layers. To fry oysters successfully, have them dry before you begin operations. Drain, and lay on a cloth, with another cloth over them, to absorb moisture. Fry your fish in hot salt pork fat, if you want to have them delicious.

BAKED FISH.

Rub the fish inside and out with salt and pepper. Make a dry dressing of bread crumbs and seasoning the same as you would for poultry; stuff the fish and sew it up. Cut gashes two inches apart and lay in slices of salt pork. Dredge it with flour; put in a dripper with meat drippings or butter and a little water. Bake from one to two hours, according to size of fish.

Sauce.—One-half cupful of butter, yolks of two eggs, juice of half a lemon, saltspoonful of salt, one-

quarter saltspoonful of cayenne pepper, two small cupfuls of boiling water. Cook about five minutes, or until
a little thicker than cream. Pour around fish and
send to table.   Mrs. Walrath,
                                      Cooking School.

BAKED MUSKALLONGE.

Clean the fish nicely, leaving on both head and tail;
wash it well in salted water, and wipe the inside very
dry with a coarse towel. Make a dressing of dry bread
crumbs, little pieces of butter, pepper, salt and chopped
onions. Fill the fish as full as you can stuff it; sew it
up. Put a few thin slices of salt pork over the top;
place in a dripper, with a little water, and bake in the
oven slowly until thoroughly cooked through. Add a
very little water occasionally, to keep it from burning,
but when it is ready to take from the fire, have it dry.
This fish makes a very tempting appearance served on
a large platter.   "Saints' Rest,"
                                   Long Lake, Wis.

BOILED MUSKALLONGE.

Clean and dry your fish thoroughly. Sew it up in
a cloth, and boil in salted water until perfectly cooked.
Roll it out on a large platter; cover the top with rings
of hard boiled eggs. Serve with drawn butter, into
which hard boiled eggs have been sliced.
                                   "Saints' Rest,"
                                   Long Lake, Wis.

BROILED OYSTERS.

Dry large select oysters on a cloth; then broil on a

greased wire broiler for a minute; have a little melted butter, pepper and salt ready; pour over and serve.

F. B. G.

BROOK TROUT.

Salt and pepper the fish inside and out (after they have been wiped very dry). Fry nice slices of salt pork; when crisp, take from the pan; keep hot to garnish your fish platter. Roll the trout in flour or corn meal, and fry in the hot pork fat until thoroughly cooked through and of a deep brown color. Put on a hot platter, with the slices of pork on the outer edge.

Mrs. Geo. C. Ginty.

CLAM CHOWDER—No. 1.

Wash fifty clams thoroughly, and put in a kettle with a dipper of water. Boil enough to open; save the brine; cut the heads off the clams and chop fine; fry to a nice brown a slice of salt pork cut up in little pieces. To a dipper of water add one and one-half bowlfuls of sliced potatoes, one and one-half good-sized onions, pepper and salt. Let boil until tender; add a little more water, if needed; then add the clams and liquor, one cupful of milk, the fried pork, and two powdered crackers; put the clams in before stirring the potatoes; take out the pieces of pork before serving. After all the ingredients are in, let it boil up once.

Mrs. Hiram Allen,
New Jersey.

CLAM CHOWDER—No. 2.

The clams used for this chowder should be " Soft Shell" or " Slim Necks " (never use " Quahaugs"). The proper kind are put up in cans on the coast of Maine, and may be purchased at any first-class grocery store. Of course, clams in the shell are better, but these serve the purpose nicely. Pare and slice thin one dozen fair-sized potatoes ; slice thin one pound of clean salt pork and place in an iron kettle over the fire until the fat is drawn ; remove the scraps; to the fat add a layer of sliced potatoes, then one of clams, and one onion, chopped fine; when all are in, add one pint of water, salt and pepper. Boil until the potatoes are cooked ; then add one quart of milk and one-half a dozen common crackers split. Let this come a boil. Remove and serve. One can of clams will be sufficient.

J. H. GRAFTON,
Winona, Minn.

CODFISH (Baked).

Soak one pint of codfish picked up into shreds. After it has soaked a few hours, simmer it on the stove until tender; drain off the water, make the fish as dry as possible, and add to it one pint of mashed potatoes, three eggs, well beaten, one pint of milk, a good lump of butter. Mix all together, and bake three-quarters of an hour. Mrs. DAISY GROSSMAN.

CODFISH BALLS.

Take a large bowlful of picked up codfish which has simmered on the stove until perfectly tender, drain it very dry with your hands, or press with the back of an iron spoon ; put this into a bowlful and a half of hot mashed potatoes ; add one egg (not beaten), a piece of butter size of a small egg, pepper and salt, if it requires it; mix up well, and roll into egg-shaped balls. Just before you fry, roll in flour; have your lard very hot and as much as you would to fry cakes; they will come to the top (if the lard is good), when you can roll them over with a fork to brown on the other side; drain as you take them out, so they will not be greasy.

Mrs. Geo. C. Ginty.

CODFISH IN CREAM.

Pick the fish up fine, and let it simmer on the back of the stove two or three hours; pour off the water; add milk, a piece of butter, a couple of eggs well beaten, and a little flour stirred up in cold milk; stir until the proper thickness, and serve with rings of hard boiled egg over the top (use cream instead of milk, if you have it, and not quite so much butter).

Mrs. L. C. Stanley.

CREAM LOAF OYSTERS.

One loaf of bread, two tablespoonfuls of butter, one quart of cream, three tablespoonfuls of flour, one-half cupful of cold milk, three pints of oysters. Bake a loaf of bread in a round two-quart basin; when two or three days old cut out the heart of the bread, being careful not to break the crust. Rub the crumbs fine, and dry them for a few minutes in the oven. Fry three cupfuls of them in two tablespoonfuls of butter. As soon as they begin to look golden or crisp, they are done (it takes about two minutes over a hot fire, stirring all the time). Put one quart of cream to boil; when it boils, stir in three tablespoonfuls of flour, which has been mixed with the cold milk. Cook eight minutes; season

well with salt and pepper. Put a layer of sauce into
the loaf from which you took the crumbs, then a layer
of oysters, pepper and salt; then another layer of sauce
and one of *fried crumbs;* continue this until the loaf is
nearly full. Have the last layer a thick one of crumbs.
Bake slowly half an hour. Garnish your dish around
the loaf with celery sprigs and send to table.

MRS. GRUNDY.

CREAM OYSTERS.

Put one quart of cream and fifty oysters in separate
kettles to heat (oysters in their own liquor). Let them
come to a boil; when sufficiently cooked, skim; take
out of the liquid and keep hot. Put cream and liquid
together; season to taste, and thicken with powdered
cracker; when sufficiently thick, stir in oysters, and
serve at once.   MRS. A. HOFFMAN.

FISH À LA CREAME.

In this case you make the sauce first, or while your
fish is boiling.

Cream Sauce.—One pint of hot cream, one heaping
tablespoonful of butter, one heaping tablespoonful of
flour, one-half teaspoonful of salt, one-half saltspoonful
of pepper; heat the cream over hot water; put the butter in a granite saucepan, and stir until it melts and
bubbles (do not brown it); add the dry flour and stir
quickly, until well mixed; add one-third of the cream;
let it boil, and stir in the rest of the cream gradually,
to have it perfectly smooth; then add salt and pepper.

While you are making this sauce, have a white fish,
weighing about four pounds, boiling or steaming until

tender. Remove all the bones, and pick the fish up in small pieces. Take a platter, from which the fish is to be served, place on it first a layer of fish (salt and pepper it), then a layer of the cream sauce, until all the fish and sauce are used. Spread over the top a cupful of cracker crumbs, moistened with butter. Pin a strip of wet muslin around the edge of your platter; set in a dripper of hot water, and bake until slightly brown.

MRS. WALRATH,

Cooking School.

FRIED OYSTERS—No. 1.

Wash the oysters, drain and season with salt and pepper; let them dry between two layers of cloth; beat the eggs in which you dip them; then roll them in cracker crumbs, and fry in hot lard or half lard and half butter; drain them as you take them out. If you have but a few to fry, roll them twice in the egg and cracker; always have your cracker crumbs seasoned. If you have a large company to partake of the oysters, you can fry them the day before you need them; have them in large dripping pans and put them in a *very hot* oven a few minutes before you serve. No one would know that they were not fried just before serving.

MRS. GEO. C. GINTY.

FRIED OYSTERS—No. 2.

Use the largest and best oysters; lay them in rows upon a clean cloth and press another upon them to absorb the moisture; have ready several beaten eggs, and in another dish some rolled crackers with pepper and salt. Heat enough butter in the frying-pan to entirely cover the oysters; dip the oysters first into butter, then into the cracker, rolling them over that they may be well covered; drop into the frying-pan and fry quickly to a light brown. Serve warm. I always boil my cooking butter and let it cool before using.

Mrs. C. P. BARKER.

MACKEREL (Salt) BROILED.

Soak in sour milk twenty-four hours, *skin side* up, and, after drying thoroughly, broil over a good bed of coals on a wire broiler. Spread butter over the top and set in the oven a minute for the butter to melt—or melt the butter and pour over the fish.

OYSTER CREAM.

Take a quart of milk, let it come to a boil, then drop in one pint of solid meat oysters, salt and pepper, stir gently until hot, but don't boil. Skim out the oysters into a hot earthen dish. Have ready one teacupful of oyster crackers, rolled, sifted and mixed with the yolks of three well-beaten eggs and just cold milk enough to stir smooth; stir this into the milk with half cupful of butter, let it simmer and last of all stir in the whites of the three eggs beaten to a stiff froth. Place three or four oysters in each cup and fill a little more than half full of the cream. Serve as first course at a lunch, with a slice of bread.

Mrs. HANNAH IRWIN,
Green Bay, Wis.

OYSTER FRITTERS.

Make a batter of the yolks of two eggs beaten well,

half a cupful of milk or water, one tablespoonful of olive oil, a good pinch of salt and one cupful of flour or more (have it almost as stiff as a drop batter); when ready to use add the whites of the eggs beaten to a stiff froth. Boil the oysters until the liquor flows freely. Drain very dry. Use the liquor (if you like the fish taste) as part of the fluid for the batter. Dip each oyster in the batter and fry until brown in hot lard, or take two oysters to each fritter, as you may like them large.

OYSTER ROYAL.

One pint of new milk, a piece of butter the size of a large egg, pepper and salt to taste; put three pints of oysters without their liquor in this, let it boil and thicken it with two tablespoonfuls of flour. Serve on toast.

PICKLED OYSTERS.

Cook a quart of oysters in their own liquor until plump or swelled; skim out the oysters, add to the liquor one-half cupful of good cider vinegar; when it boils up skim it and add eight whole pepper corns, eight allspice berries, eight cloves, a pinch of cayenne pepper and a teaspoonful of salt. Boil six minutes; pour over the oysters, and when cool seal up in glass jars. Keep in a cool dark place. They will keep a couple of weeks.   MRS. GEO. C. GINTY.

SCALLOPED OYSTERS.

Roll fine a dozen crackers; have ready butter, pepper, salt and oysters; grease a shallow dish with

butter, sprinkle in a layer of cracker crumbs, then a
layer of oysters, salt, pepper, and small pieces of good
butter; repeat this until your dish is filled having the
last layer crumbs; wet with a *little* oyster juice or
cream (most of these dishes are spoiled by being wet or
mushy). Bake half an hour.

SCALLOPED SALMON.

One can of salmon, drain all the juice or oil from it
and mince fine ; one-half cupful of bread crumbs, one
cupful of milk, boiled ; mix a tablespoonful of flour
and two of butter together; pour the boiling milk over
this and make a paste stirring so that it will be
smooth ; pour this over the salmon which should be in a
shallow dish. Shake the bread crumbs over the top
and bake in a moderate oven three quarters of an hour.

MRS. WM. O'NIEL.

TURBOT.

Boil whitefish about fifteen minutes, pick the meat
up quite fine.

Dressing.—One quart of sweet milk boil and add
one-fourth pound of butter, salt, pepper and a few celery
or parsley leaves chopped fine ; thicken with flour to
consistency of thick cream ; put in buttered dish a layer
of fish, then one of the dressing ; repeat until the dish
is full ; cover top layer with rolled crackers and bake
half an hour.   MRS. WILL TALLMADGE.

WHITEFISH (Broiled).

Clean and wipe very dry ; cut down lengthwise
close to the back-bone so that you may lay the fish flat

on the broiler; broil on a wire broiler moving up and down often, that the fish may not burn; have melted butter, pepper and salt ready to pour over the top. Serve at once.   Always broil the flesh side first, the skin side just enough to crisp it; garnish your dish with slices of broiled salt pork.   Mrs. Geo. C. Ginty.

MEMORANDA.

MEMORANDA.

Some hae meat that canna eat,
And some would eat that want it ;
But we hae meat, and we can eat.
Sae let the Lord be thankit,
—BURNS.

MEATS AND POULTRY.

Use dry dressing for all poultry, fowls and game. Bread crumbs rubbed fine (chopping the crusts), season with salt, pepper and savory, onions, sage or anything you like, put little pieces of butter through the crumbs as you use them. The juices from the fowl will moisten the dressing sufficiently and it will not taste like paste.

When you broil or fry salt pork, take it from the broiler or frying pan and dip it in sweet milk, return to the fire, repeat this occasionally until the pork is done. It makes it very sweet and delicate.

We have not given the usual receipts in this department, but a few choice dishes, a little out of the general order of things, taking it for granted that our readers can roast, broil, bake, stew and fry in the usual conventional manner.

A NICE "PICK-UP."

Chop cold meat fine; half fill a pudding-dish with boiled maccaroni, also chopped ; lay the meat next ; pour over it a cupful of drawn butter mixed with one-half cupful of strained tomato juice; strew with bread crumbs and bake. Rice may be substituted for maccaroni.

BEEF LOAF.

Four pounds of raw beef, three-fourths pound of salt pork, chopped fine, three-fourths cupful of crackers, crushed fine, two eggs, four and one-half teaspoonfuls of salt, four teaspoonfuls of pepper, one tablespoonful of butter, three tablespoonfuls of milk. Work the mixture up well in a chopping tray, pack in a mold or pan, set in a dripping pan of hot water, bake one and one-quarter hours. Keep the pan full of boiling water.

Mrs. W. E. Tallmadge.

BEEFSTEAK LOAF.

Three pounds of round steak, chopped fine; eleven soda crackers, rolled fine; six eggs, well beaten; butter the size of two eggs, salt, pepper and savory to taste; rub all together; bake in a loaf or bar one and one-half hours. Make the day before you want it as it cuts down better in thin slices.

Mrs. G. C. Ginty.

BEEFSTEAK PUDDING.

One and one-half pounds of juicy round steak, cut in square pieces, take out all gristle and skin, leave a little fat, season highly with pepper and salt, make a suet crust, grease a quart bowl, roll the crust one-half an inch thick, lay in the bowl; in this put your meat; when full, pour in one-half cupful of water, lay the paste all over the top, leaving no cracks through which the gravy can boil out; tie in a floured cloth; boil two hours constantly; when done remove the cloth, run a thin knife around the edge, and turn on a hot dish carefully.

Suet Paste.—Chop one-half pound of the best suet very fine; remove the fibers; rub the suet into one pound of flour; add one teaspoonful of salt and mix it with one-half pint of ice water; roll, put on a little butter in flakes, rolling it in as usual. Some add one teaspoonful of baking powder.

Mrs. M. Harvey,
Hamilton, Ont.

BOILED CORNED BEEF.

Soak over night if very salt, but if properly corned this is not necessary. Put in your kettle and cover well with hot water; let it boil gently on the back of the stove, three hours to eight pounds of meat; be sure and not let it boil fast, as it hardens the meat.

BOILED DINNER.

Boil a piece of corned-beef and a small piece of salt pork, one hour; change the water and boil again; add one chicken, give the chicken two hours to boil if old, and one if young; put your vegetables in the same pot, giving each kind the time they require; when done put the beef, pork and chicken on a platter and lay the vegetables around them. This makes a delicious dinner.

BOILED LEG OF MUTTON.

One tablespoonful of butter, one teaspoonful of onion juice; put mutton in kettle, and cook ten minutes over a hot fire, in the butter and onion juice, turning frequently; then cover with hot water; put in slice of lemon, pepper and salt; cook two and one-half hours; serve with one cupful of tomato juice, teaspoonful of butter, teaspoonful of flour, tablespoonful of vinegar, salt and pepper.   MRS. L. J. RUSK.

BROILED BEEFSTEAK AND MAITRE BUTTER.

Lay a thick tender steak upon a gridiron well greased with butter, over hot coals; sear on one side, turn immediately and sear the other, and finish cooking, turning often. Spread on the hot beef steak a maitre sauce found in catchups and sauces in this book.

CHICKEN GELATINE.

Boil one chicken in a small quantity of water until tender, take it up and strain the liquor: add to the liquor one-third package of gelatine ; after it is all dissolved, put in the meat, not chopped, but picked up : let it boil up: season with salt, a little pepper, and turn into a mold to cool.

CHICKEN PIE.

Joint the chicken, put in a kettle, cover with water, and boil until tender, then cut in small pieces, removing the bones, line a dish with pastry, made of six cupfuls of flour, one of lard, one cupful of water and one-half teaspoonful of salt : sprinkle some flour over the bottom crust : place in the chicken ; sprinkle salt, pepper and more flour over the top of chicken, also bits of butter ; pour as much gravy as necessary over the whole; then spread on the remainder of the crust: put bits of butter over the top and bake one-half hour.

                              MRS. WM. MARTIN.

CORNED LEG OF MUTTON.

Have your butcher put a leg of mutton in brine, for three days; then boil until well done. This sliced cold, is very good for supper or lunch.

DEVILED HAM.

1 pint of ham, chopped very fine, yolks of four hard boiled eggs; rub smooth as possible, with one-half cupful of olive oil or butter; pepper and mustard to taste; mix thoroughly with ham until it forms a paste, with two-thirds cupful of vinegar. Nice for sandwiches.

DEVILED VEAL.

Thick part of a leg of veal chopped fine, two slices of salt pork chopped fine, two slices of bread crumbed. three eggs, one pint of milk, pepper and salt. Bake two and one-half hours; serve cold, cut in slices.

Miss MARIETTA J. CARY,

Binghamton. N. Y.

ENGLISH HUNTER'S BEEF.

A round of beef, twenty pounds from the hind-quarter. Place in large wooden bowl, one and one-half pounds brown sugar, one pound salt, one ounce cinnamon, one ounce allspice, one ounce cloves, one ounce nutmeg. and one ounce saltpetre. Rub these ingredients into the meat and let it stand for three weeks, turning the meat every second day in the mixture. Wipe all spices off, place in a deep dripper, cover closely with paste made of flour and water, and bake in the oven four or five hours.

Mrs. E. PATTON.

ENGLISH POT PIE OF BEEF.

Take nearly two pounds of round stake, cut into finger lengths, flour lightly, put a three-quart iron sauce pan on the stove, when hot, drop in fat of steak, then the meat, let it fry very quickly, then peel medium sized carrot, onion and turnip, cut in small, regular sized pieces, drop them in sauce pan, stir around quickly and pour over two cupfuls of boiling water, season with teaspoonful of salt, one-fourth teaspoonful of pepper, cover tight, when it comes to the boil, set back on the stove and let simmer nearly two hours, then take a teacupful of fine chopped suet, two scant cupfuls of flour, a level teaspoonful of salt, mix lightly in a bowl, make a hole in the center and pour in half a cupful of cold water, and mix with a knife, adding a few drops of water, to bind the crumbs, roll out quickly, an inch thick, and a little larger than lid of sauce pan, taste your gravy, to see if seasoned enough, lay the dough on top of meat and vegetables, place on the hottest part of stove a minute, then let simmer one hour; when done cut the crust like pie, and lay around the meat. Do not let it stop simmering or the crust will be heavy.

MRS. BISHOP,

New Jersey.

FRESH MEAT GRIDDLES.

Chop bits of any cold roast meat; season with pepper and salt; make a griddle batter; put a spoonful on a well-buttered griddle; then a spoonful of the chopped meat, and on this, another spoonful of the batter. When cooked on one side, turn ; when done, send to the table hot. They are nice for breakfast or lunch.

Mrs. L. H. Cushing.

FRICASSEED CHICKEN.

Cut up chicken ; put on to boil in a little water; season with salt and pepper ; cook till tender, taking care it does not boil dry, when done, pour on one pint of thick sweet cream, place in a hot dish, and serve.

Mrs. F. M. Buzzle.

FRITTADILLA.

One pint finely chopped roast beef, or scraps of cold meat of different kinds, one pint dry bread crumbs, one tablespoonful of onion, chopped fine ; soak bread crumbs in water, and squeeze dry in a cloth ; put a tablespoonful of butter in a spider ; melt it; then put the onions in it two or three minutes; then put in bread crumbs and meat. Heat all through, and mix all together, with two well-beaten eggs. Make into little cakes; fry in butter till brown. Mrs. L. S. Searles,

Stillwater, Minn.

HAMBURG STEAK.

One pound chopped lean steak, yolk of one egg two oyster crackers, pepper and salt to taste; fry with a tablespoonful of butter and three drops of onion juice, to be made into little flat cakes before frying.

KIDNEY STEW.

Soak the kidneys two or three hours in salt and water, then stew till tender ; slice very thin in small pieces, and put in a stew pan, with three tablespoonfuls of butter, dredge in two tablespoonfuls of flour, then add one cupful of sweet cream and one cupful of the soup it was boiled in (strained) and chop or slice in small pieces one hard boiled egg and add with two tablespoonfuls of sherry wine. Serve. Use only the best part of the kidney. Mrs. Wm. O'Niel.

MEAT PIE.

Cut cold roast beef or veal in small pieces, an inch in size; put into stew-pan; cover with water; add good-sized piece butter, one large onion cut fine; season with pepper and salt; boil until onion is tender; thicken the gravy with flour.

Paste for Meat Pie.—Make the same as for baking-powder biscuit, except adding more butter.

Mrs. L. H. Cushing.

MOCK GOOSE.

Take two pounds of round steak, pound well, lay on table; take small bowl of cold mashed potatoes, a small onion chopped very fine, pepper, salt, and a sprinkle of sage, and a small piece of butter: mix well together, spread on steak; roll it up and fasten firm with string or skewers; put small pieces of salt pork around it and a little butter; keep well basted, and bake two hours; serve with nice brown gravy.

Mrs. J. Kyle.

MOCK SWEET BREADS.

One pound of uncooked lean veal; cook in salted water, with slice of onion; then put it into cold water to whiten it; make one cupful of white sauce (found in catchups and sauces in this book); season with salt, pepper and celery salt; put the veal and one-half cupful of mushrooms into the sauce; heat over boiling water; cut the mushrooms into quarters; take from fire when heated; add one teaspoonful of lemon juice and one well-beaten egg; garnish with potato.

MUTTON PIES.

A little more than one pound of lean mutton cut into small pieces; put into basin and sprinkle over it one teaspoonful salt, three-fourths teaspoonful of pepper, and one-half teacupful of water, mix thoroughly.

Paste.—One-fourth pound suet chopped fine, three-fourths teacupful of milk, put on to boil with the suet, add pinch of salt and good three-fourths pound flour, when milk and suet have boiled, strain over flour and mix by hand, roll in thin pieces the thickness of your hand, press on the sides of a circular tin about three inches in diameter, fill with the meat, cover with a circular piece of the paste with a small hole cut in the center, brush over with milk and bake half an hour.

Miss Christie McDougall.

OYSTER DRESSING FOR TURKEY OR CHICKEN.

Place a quantity of stale bread crumbs in the oven; when brown and crisp place on bread board; roll fine with rolling-pin; add to the crumbs one pint of oysters, one-half cupful of butter, salt and pepper; a little sage may be used, or a small onion.

Mrs. Hiram Allen,
New York.

PORK AND BEANS.

One quart of beans, one pound of salt pork, one
tablespoonful of molasses, one of salt, one teaspoonful
of mustard, one-quarter teaspoonful of soda ; soak the
beans over night, in the morning rinse in cold water,
put on to boil in cold water with the pork ; let them
boil fifteen minutes; take from the fire and drain the
beans in a colander; rinse again in cold water ; put
the pork in a dish with the beans ready for baking and
mix the molasses, salt, mustard and soda with a quart
of boiling water and pour over them : bake ten hours;
add boiling water when required.   This sounds like a
great undertaking, but is not when one is about the
kitchen, and they are so nice that it pays to use this
receipt.   MRS. J. C. OUTHWAITE,
                                   Depere, Wis.

POTTED LIVER.

Boil beef and any kind of liver, until you can run a
straw through it; remove all bits of fat and sinews;
chop very fine.   Then melt as much good butter as you
can spare; spices to taste; pepper and salt.   Pour hot
over the liver; mix thoroughly together; put in jar.
This will keep a long time, and makes good sandwiches.   MRS. M. HARVEY,
                                   Hamilton, Ont.

PRESSED CHICKEN.

Two chickens boiled in as little water as possible
until tender : pick the meat from the bones, then put it
back into the kettle, adding plenty of butter, pepper and
salt; heat it thoroughly : slice hard boiled egg and

place in the bottom of a dish; pour it in hot, and place a weight upon it and put it away to cool.

PRESSED MEAT.

Boil a piece of fresh mutton, beef or veal, until perfectly tender; take out the bones and gristle; chop fine; add salt and pepper; if very lean add butter. Pack it solid while warm, and slice when cold.

Mrs. L. H. CUSHING.

ROAST GOOSE OR DUCK.

Remove all the fat possible; wash, and dry with a cloth the inside of the fowl for the dressing; take cold mashed potatoes, a little onion chopped very fine, a sprinkling of sage, pepper, salt and a little butter; mix well together; stuff the inside, and also at the neck of the goose or duck; sew all firmly up and tie in shape; roast slowly for two or three hours, basting and turning often. Have the giblets stewed tender, chopped fine, and put in gravy. The fowls must be a rich brown and juicy.

Mrs. E. PATTON.

ROAST SIRLOIN.

"There is one instant in the existence of roast sirloin when it is fit food for men, before which it is suited to carniverous beasts and after which it should be relegated to the mugwumps; when the outside is crisp, and brown, and well done, and the inside is juicy, and red, and rare, the whole being as hot as a Puritan's holy rage at Anabaptists, and tender as his conscience. For this instant the roast is an epic; before, it is tradition, and after, it is prose."

OLD RECEIPT.

ROAST VEAL AND TONGUE.

Take a small leg of veal; remove the large bones; place a small pickled tongue, that has been boiled and skinned, in the space left by the removal of the bone; fasten firmly with skewers; put salt and pepper on top, and a thin slice of salt pork; roast two hours in oven; slice horizontally when cold.   Mrs. J. Kyle.

ROLLED BEAFSTEAK.

Take a slice of round steak an inch thick; pound well; season with salt and pepper; then spread a dressing, the same as for turkey, on the top; roll it up and fasten with twine; plunge it in boiling water, to close the pores; then place in covered dish and set in a kettle of hot water, boil for one hour; then take out and put in dripping pan, laying slices of salt pork on top; pour over it the juice boiled out, and bake one hour. This is delicious sliced cold.

SCALLOPED TURKEY.

Cut the turkey into small pieces; use a layer of this, with bits of dressing and a little gravy if you have it; next a very thin layer of bread crumbs or rolled cracker, with a little butter; then a layer of meat, dressing, etc.; finish with bread crumbs. Should sufficient dressing be used, no other seasoning will be needed, otherwise salt and pepper must be used with each layer. Should it lack moisture, add a beaten egg in a small cup of milk. Bake from thirty to forty-five minutes, according to size of dish and temperature of oven.

SCOTCH HOTCH-POTCH.

Cut neck or breast of lamb in pieces, put in stew-pan, cover with water; add pepper and salt: stew half an hour; add young onions, carrots, white turnips and potatoes; if necessary, add more water; twenty minutes before serving, add one quart of green peas shelled.

STEWED BEEFSTEAK.

Two pounds of round steak, pound until tender; cut in slices; dredge with flour, pepper and salt, and roll in tight rolls; lay in a stew pan with a few cloves, and a scrap of nutmeg: cover with water, and stew three hours.   MRS. E. PATTON.

VEAL BIRDS.

Slices of veal cut from the loin. Remove bones, skin and fat, pound it until it is one-fourth inch thick; cut into pieces, four inches square; take little pieces trimmed off, with pork and chop fine; take one-half as much sifted cracker crumbs as you have meat; season highly with salt, pepper, thyme, lemon, cayenne, and onion; moisten with one egg beaten to the consistency of soap-suds or stock; spread the mixture on each slice and roll over and fasten with tooth picks; dredge with flour, fry in butter until a nice brown, then half cover with cream and simmer twenty minutes. Remove the picks; serve on toast, after thickening the cream with flour.   MRS. WALRATH,

Cooking School.

VEAL CHOPS FRIED.

Dip the chops in beaten egg, then in fine cracker

crumbs; season with pepper, salt and a little sifted sage;
fry the chop in hot lard for twenty minutes. They
should be a rich brown.   MRS. KYLE.

VEAL OMELET.

Three pounds of veal chopped fine, one-half pound
of salt pork chopped fine, four soda crackers rolled fine,
one teacupful of sweet cream, seasoned with salt, pepper, sage and thyme; mix all together; make in a
loaf; bake three hours; baste often, at first with butter,
then as it cooks use its own dripping.

MRS. J. C. MITCHELL,

Chicago, Ill.

VEAL POT-PIE.

Take two or three pounds of veal (chicken may be
used), place in a quart of cold water: season with salt
and pepper: take nearly a quart of flour, make into
biscuit, using baking powder: when veal is tender drop
in a large piece of butter; put in biscuit; cover tightly;
cook twenty minutes; take veal and biscuit from kettle,
and thicken gravy with flour; pour over all and serve
in a hot dish.   MRS. F. A. RECKARD.

BRINE FOR BEEF (Celebrated).

One hundred pounds of meat: Six gallons of water,
nine pounds of salt (half coarse), three pounds of brown
sugar, one quart of molasses, three ounces of saltpeter,
one ounce of pearl-ash: boil and skim. Pour over
meat hot.   MRS. DANIEL WHITNEY,

Green Bay, Wis.

A dinner lubricates business.
—JOHNSON.

VEGETABLES.

TO SERVE WITH DIFFERENT MEATS, GAME, POULTRY, FISH, ETC.

With Roast Beef.—Potatoes, squash, boiled rice or macaroni, pickles, or any vegetables that are in season.

With Roast Mutton.—Mashed potatoes, mashed turnips, boiled onions and currant jelly.

With Roast Lamb.—Potatoes, green peas, turnips, string beans, corn, summer squash, mint sauce.

With Roast Veal.—Mashed potatoes, spinach, parsnips, asparagus, sweet potatoes, horseradish.

With Roast Pork.—Potatoes, onions, squash or sweet potatoes, tomatoes, boiled rice and apple sauce.

With Roast Venison.—Mashed potatoes, squash, onions, turnips and currant jelly.

With Roast Turkey.—Potatoes, squash or sweet potatoes, onions, celery and cranberry sauce or jelly.

With Roast Chicken.—Potatoes, onions, squash, or any green vegetable in season, celery and currant jelly.

With Roast Goose.—Mashed potatoes, onions, squash, baked macaroni or boiled rice, apple sauce.

With Roast Ducks.—Same as for goose.

With Birds of all Kinds.—Potatoes, squash, onions, celery, macaroni and currant jelly.

With Boiled Mutton.—Mashed potatoes. mashed turnips, baked macaroni, currant jelly.

With Boiled Lamb.—Potatoes, green peas. asparagus. spinach, white turnips.

With Boiled Corned Beef.—Potatoes, cabbage, parsnips, beets and turnips.

With Boiled Fowl.—Mashed potatoes, turnips, parsnips, macaroni, currant jelly, oyster or celery sauce.

With Boiled Turkey.—Oyster or celery sauce, potatoes, turnips, parsnips, lettuce and cranberry sauce.

With Boiled Veal.—Mashed potatoes, spinach or dandelion, macaroni and cheese, horseradish.

With Calfs' Head.—Potatoes, parsnips, dandelions or spinach, horseradish.

With Beefsteak.—Potatoes, squash, tomatoes, or any vegetables that are in season.

With Lamb or Mutton Chops.—Potatoes, both kinds, turnips, tomato sauce or lettuce, pickles.

With Veal Steak.—Potatoes, both kinds, spinach or lettuce, horseradish.

With Baked Fish.—Mashed potatoes, squash or sweet potatoes, lettuce, cranberry sauce.

With Broiled or Fried Fish.—Potatoes, turnips, squash, tomato sauce, lemon or horseradish.

Serenely full, the epicure would say.
Fate cannot harm me, I have dined to-day.
—SIDNEY SMITH.

ASPARAGUS.

Wash clean; cut off the white part, except a mere end; put into slightly salted boiling water, boil five minutes, pour off water, add more boiling hot; boil till tender; then add butter, pepper and salt; just before serving stir in a thickening made of one teaspoonful of flour mixed up with cold milk. One-half cupful of cream improves it. Or, boil in salted water till tender; season with butter, pepper and cream; pour over nicely toasted bread.

BAKED CORN.

One can of corn, two beaten eggs, one tablespoonful of sugar, butter, pepper and salt to taste; one pint of milk, one tablespoonful of flour; bake half an hour.

BEET GREENS.

Look over carefully to see that no bugs or worms remain; wash very clean, but do not separate roots from leaves; fill dinner-pot half full of salted boiling water; add beets; boil three-quarters of an hour; take out and drain so as to get out all the water. Dish, and dress with butter, pepper and salt, if needed. Serve hot, with vinegar.

BEETS.

Remove leaves, wash clean, and boil in plenty of

water; if young, two hours will boil them, if old four hours. Try with fork to see when tender. Take out, drop into a pan of cold water, and slip off the skin with the hands; slice, place in a dish, season with butter, pepper and salt; set over boiling water to heat thoroughly, and serve hot with or without vinegar. Or, after beets are boiled and skinned, mash with boiled potatoes, and season with butter, pepper and salt; serve hot.

BOILED CAULIFLOWER.

Choose the close and white cauliflower; trim off all outside leaves; cut the flowers from the stalk and let them lie in salt and water for half an hour; then put into boiling water, adding a little salt, and boil briskly for twenty minutes; when tender, drain; add milk and butter, or cream, a little pepper; let come to a boil, and serve hot.

BOILED CORN.

Put the well-cleaned ears in salted boiling water; boil an hour; take out of the water and send to table hot. To be eaten with butter, salt and pepper.

BOILED DINNER.

Wash a nice piece of corned beef and put in a dinner-pot with just enough boiling water to cover it; boil slowly at least four hours; if beets are old, put them in to boil when you do the meat; put in other vegetables in the following order: Turnips cut in quarters require about two hours to boil; cabbage cut in quarters one hour and a half; carrots and parsnips three-quarters of an hour; potatoes half an hour. Boil all together; when done, take up in separate dishes, and lastly the meat. Slice the carrots into a sauce-pan; add half a cupful of cream or milk, a small piece of butter, salt and pepper; let them come to a boil and serve hot. When the meat and beets have been put on to boil, clean the other vegetables and let them remain in cold water till needed.

BOILED MACARONI.

Boil the macaroni in salted water until soft; drain. Make a sauce of butter and bread crumbs warmed together; when warm, stir in sweet cream or milk; pour this sauce on the macaroni while hot.

Mrs. B. Himmelsbach.

BOILED ONIONS.

Peel and wash; boil twenty minutes; pour off water; add boiling water, with a little salt; let boil till quite tender; add a cupful of milk, and boil ten minutes longer; drain; season with butter, pepper and salt, and a little cream. if you have it.

CORN DODGERS.

Twelve ears of corn, scraped; one pint of cream, three eggs, small teaspoonful of saleratus, flour enough to thicken like batter cakes. If you have not cream, take milk and melted butter; salt. Mrs. Ernst Funke,

Oconto, Wis.

CORN OYSTERS—No. 1.

One cupful of flour, one-half cupful of butter, three tablespoonfuls of milk, two teaspoonfuls of salt, one-

fourth teaspoonful of pepper, one pint of grated corn;
pour the corn on the flour, and beat well; then add the
other ingredients, and beat rapidly for three minutes;
have fat in the frying pan to the depth of about two
inches; when smoking hot put in the batter by the
spoonful, holding the spoon close to the fat, and the
shape of the oyster will be good; fry about five
minutes.

CORN OYSTERS—No. 2.

Six nice plump ears of sweet corn; grate, beat one
egg, add one tablespoonful each of flour and sweet
milk; stir into grated corn, drop the mixture, a spoonful in a place into hot lard, and fry brown.

Mrs. A. J. Cady,

Rockford, Ill.

CORN OYSTERS (Green)—No. 3.

Six large ears corn grated, three eggs, three or four
grated crackers, one-half cupful of milk, salt and
pepper to taste. Fry on the pancake griddle with
butter.   Mrs. A. Hoffman.

CORN OYSTERS—No. 4.

One can of corn, two eggs, two tablespoonfuls of
flour, two tablespoonfuls of sweet milk, salt and pepper
to taste. Fry as batter cakes.   Mrs. Waters.

CREAMED CABBAGE.

Slice as for cold slaw; put in sauce-pan with water
enough to keep from burning; add pepper and salt, and
a lump of butter; cover and cook till tender. Just
before dishing up, add one cupful of cream.

DANDELIONS.

Cut off the leaves, pick over carefully, wash in several waters, put into boiling water, boil one hour, drain well, add salted boiling water and boil two hours; when done, take up with a fork and drain; melt butter and pour over them; add more salt if needed or boil with a piece of salt pork, omitting the butter.

DRIED CORN.

Wash, and soak over night in cold water; when softened, cook five or ten minutes in water in which it was soaked, adding as soon as boiling, two tablespoonfuls of butter, a little salt and pepper; cream if desired.

DUCHESS POTATOES.

Five boiled potatoes, cold, five heaping dessert-spoonfuls of flour, one-half teaspoonful of baking powder, two eggs, a good half cupful of milk, a little salt; grate the potatoes; add lightly, stirring with a fork, other ingredients; drop from spoon into boiling lard; fry until the balls are of a rich brown. They are very nice.   MRS. A. HOFFMAN.

EGG PLANT.

Peel, slice and boil until tender; mash and season with pepper and salt; roll crackers or dry bread and stir into it until very thick; make into patties; fry in hot lard or with a piece of salt pork.

ESCALOPED CAULIFLOWER.

Boil until tender, clip into clusters and pack into a buttered pudding-dish, stems downward; beat a cupful of bread crumbs to a soft paste with two tablespoonfuls of melted butter, and three of cream or milk; season with pepper and salt; add a well beaten egg and with this cover the cauliflower; cover the dish closely and bake six minutes in a quick oven; remove cover, and brown. Serve hot.

ESCALOPED POTATOES.

Peel; steam; when done, slice same as for frying. Butter an earthen dish and put in a layer of potatoes, and season with salt, pepper, butter and a bit of onion chopped fine; sprinkle with a little flour; continue this until the dish is filled; let stand half an hour; then pour over one cupful of milk. Bake thirty-five minutes.   Mrs. W. Squires.

ESCALOPED TOMATOES.

Peel, and cut in slices rather thick; line a deep dish with the tomatoes and sprinkle bread crumbs thickly over them; season with butter, pepper, salt and a little white sugar; add another layer of tomatoes with the seasoning, and so on until the dish is full. Let the tomatoes be uppermost, with a bit of butter on each slice; dust with the bread crumbs; cover the dish and let them bake for half an hour; remove cover, and let them brown.

FRIED CABBAGE.

Cut the cabbage very fine; have ready a frying-pan in which a slice or two of salt pork has been fried; while it is smoking hot drop in the cabbage, stirring briskly until quite tender. After taken from the stove stir in one-half cupful of cream, and three tablespoonfuls of vinegar. Send to table immediately.

FRIED HOMINY.

Cut cold, boiled hominy in slices, and fry in butter until a nice brown. Serve with syrup, or butter and sugar.

FRIED ONIONS.

Peel and wash, cut in slices; boil half an hour; drain; fry in butter or salt pork fat; stir often; season with pepper and salt. Serve hot.

FRIED PARSNIPS.

Wash, scrape, and cut lengthwise; boil in slightly salted water till tender; drain, and fry in butter. Parsnips are nice mashed and seasoned with butter, pepper and salt.

GREEN CORN FRITTERS.

Twelve ears of corn, grated; four eggs, tablespoonful of butter, salt, very little flour; fry like griddle cakes.

GREEN PEAS.

Shell and wash lightly. Cook half an hour in salted water; add a lump of sugar unless fresh from the vines; drain; add cream, or milk and butter, pepper and salt. Let them remain on top of stove till the milk is hot; serve. Some stir in a thickening made of one teaspoonful of flour mixed up with cold milk.

HOMINY.

Soak two cupfuls of hominy in cold water over night; in the morning, put into rice boiler and let cook three or four hours; add water as needed. Salt just before taking from the stove.   Serve with cream and sugar.

KOHL-RABI.

Peel, cut into slices about half an inch thick; cover with water and boil about two hours; drain, fry in butter like parsnips; season with salt and pepper; or mash and season.

LIMA BEANS.

Shell them; wash in cold water. Boil them one hour; when done drain off the water; season with salt and pepper, cream or butter.   Serve hot.

Dried beans should be soaked over night, and boiled two hours or longer.   Season the same as green beans.

MASHED POTATO.

Two cupfuls of mashed potato, two eggs well beaten, one tablespoonful of butter, one teaspoonful of salt, one-half cupful of boiling milk; put in buttered pudding-dish, and bake in a quick oven thirty minutes, or until the top is browned.

OKRA.

Parboil till tender with a little salt in the water, then roll in meal and fry like fish. Or, stew an equal quantity of tomatoes and tender sliced okra; stew in porcelain kettle fifteen or twenty minutes; season with butter, pepper and salt, and serve.

PARSNIP CROQUETTES.

Mash fine, cold, boiled parsnips. To six parsnips add one egg beaten light; salt, pepper and flour enough to hold them together; form into small, flat cakes, and fry brown. Mrs. W. Squires.

PARSNIP FRITTERS.

Boil five or six medium-sized parsnips till tender; mash very fine; add one-half cupful of milk, two tablespoonfuls of melted butter, two eggs, three tablespoonfuls of flour, and a little salt; beat all together; fry a delicate brown in hot drippings. Serve on a hot dish.

POTATOES AND ONIONS.

Pare and boil till done; drain; mash in the kettle until perfectly smooth; add a cupful of cream or a generous lump of butter and a cupful of milk; pepper and salt to taste; mince a medium sized onion quite fine; add to the potato and mix well; cover closely, and let cook about ten minutes. R. B. Clark.

POTATOES BAKED.

Wash clean, wipe dry, put in a moderately hot oven in a baking pan, increasing heat until the skin becomes firm and of a light brown color. If the oven is kept at the proper temperature potatoes will bake in from thirty to forty minutes, according to size. Baked potatoes should be taken from the oven and served as soon as they are done. Potatoes baked with fowl or meat of any kind are very nice. Pare and parboil, then place in the pan containing the fowl or roast; turn over when partly cooked so they may brown evenly. Peel cold baked patatoes; slice into a frying-pan; add cream, butter, pepper and salt; set on the stove and let them come to a boil; stir, and heat thoroughly.

POTATOES BAKED IN MILK.

Wash, peel and slice into cold water, and let them remain for half an hour; put into pudding dish; season with salt and pepper; add milk enough to come nearly to the top of potatoes; put into oven and bake one hour; take out and scatter bits of butter over the top and pour in half a cupful of cream; return to oven for ten minutes. Serve in the dish they are baked in.

POTATOES BOILED.

To boil either pared or unpared potatoes, put them when prepared into slightly salted boiling water, and keep them boiling until tender enough to pierce easily with a fork, then drain; sprinkle with salt; cover with a folded towel and set back on the range to dry off, and keep hot. If they have been boiled without paring, the skins can be removed before sending them to the table.

POTATO CROQUETTES.

One pint of hot mashed potato, one tablespoonful of melted butter, one-half saltspoonful of white pepper, a speck of cayenne pepper, one-half saltspoonful of salt, one-half saltspoonful of celery salt, a few drops of onion juice, yolk of one egg; mix all but the egg; beat until very light; when slightly cool, add the yolk and mix well. Rub through a sieve; make into balls; roll in fine bread crumbs, then dip in beaten egg, then roll in crumbs, and fry in hot lard.

Miss MAY WILLIAMS,
Whitewater, Wis.

POTATOES FRIED RAW.

Peel, wash, and cut in very thin slices, and put in frying-pan prepared with two tablespoonfuls of melted butter, and one of beef-drippings; season with salt; cover closely, and let them fry about thirty minutes; remove cover frequently and stir from the bottom with a knife to prevent burning.

POTATOES MASHED.

Pare and wash; put them in boiling water with a little salt. When done, drain; let them stand until perfectly dry, then mash until smooth; add milk or cream, small piece of butter, and more salt. Beat with a spoon until creamy and light.

POTATO PUFFS—No. 1.

To two cupfuls of cold, mashed potato, add two cupfuls of sweet cream, two tablespoonfuls of melted butter, two well-beaten eggs and a little salt; mix thoroughly and turn into a basin, and bake in a quick oven.

Mrs. DAISY GROSSMAN.

POTATO PUFFS—No. 2.

Mash, while hot, boiled potatoes; season well with butter, cream and salt; beat until smooth and light; while hot, shape into balls about the size of an egg; have a tin sheet well buttered and place balls on it; brush them over with a well beaten egg; put in oven and brown; when done, slip a knife under and slide them on to a hot platter; garnish with parsley, and serve immediately.

Mrs. WILLIAM IRVINE.

POTATOES WARMED.

Chop cold, boiled potatoes quite fine; season with salt and pepper; put into a hot skillet in which a tablespoonful of butter has been melted; pour in milk to nearly cover the potatoes; then put the tongs on top of the stove; set the skillet on the tongs; cover closely, and let them warm slowly until well heated through. When ready to serve, put butter cut in small pieces over the top of potatoes and dish them up lightly. Do not stir them while cooking.   ANNIE SHAVER,

New York.

SALSIFY OR OYSTER PLANT.

Wash and scrape the roots, dropping each into cold water as soon as it is cleaned; exposure to the air blackens them. Cut in pieces an inch long; put into a saucepan with hot water enough to cover them, and stew until tender. Turn off nearly all the water, and add a cupful of cold milk. Stew ten minutes after this begins to boil; put in butter cut into bits, and rolled in flour; pepper and salt to taste. Boil up once and serve. A piece of salt codfish boiled with the salsify gives it more of an oyster flavor; remove codfish before sending to the table.

SALSIFY OR VEGETABLE OYSTER.

Wash, scrape, and slice thin; cook in water enough to cover it well, until done; then add milk, butter, salt, pepper and rolled crackers, the same as for oyster soup.

SOUR KRAUT.

Wash the kraut thoroughly; boil with a piece of

fresh pork two or three hours; just before serving, sprinkle a little flour over it. Serve hot.

Mrs. B. Himmelsbach.

SPINACH.

This receipt applies to any "greens." Cook the spinach in enough salted boiling water to cover it; when tender, place in colander and drain, and chop fine afterwards; then fry it a few minutes, with a little butter, pepper and salt; serve with sliced hard boiled eggs on top. Served as a course, it is arranged as follows: Put a circle of thin slices of buttered toast (one slice for each person at the table) around the dish, on each slice put a cupful of spinach, neatly smoothed in shape; press the half of a hard boiled egg into each pile of spinach, leaving the cut part of the egg uppermost.

STEAMED CABBAGE.

Cut the cabbage very fine. Take two tablespoonfuls of butter, same of lard, one cupful of vinegar and one cupful of water; let come to a boil; add cabbage seasoned with pepper and salt; cover closely; boil very slowly for two or three hours.

Mrs. B. Himmelsbach.

STEWED CARROTS.

Cut the carrots lengthwise, and boil until perfectly tender; when done, have ready a sauce-pan with two tablespoonfuls of butter, and small cupful of cream; slice carrots into the pan; add pepper and salt; let them stew ten or fifteen minutes, stirring gently once or twice and serve in a vegetable dish.

STEWED CORN.

Shave corn off the ear, being careful not to cut into the cob, to three pints of corn, add three tablespoonfuls of butter, salt and pepper, with just enough water to cover; place in sauce pan; cover and cook slowly from one-half to three quarters of an hour; stir with a spoon often, and if necessary add more water; a few moments before it is done, add one-half cupful of sweet cream.

STEWED PARSNIPS.

Wash, scrape, and cut into slices about one-half inch thick; put into a rice boiler; add one-half cupful of water; season with salt and pepper, a tablespoonful of melted butter; cover closely, and let cook till tender. When ready to serve, add one-half cupful of sweet cream.

STRING BEANS.

String; break or cut in pieces an inch long; wash and boil in plenty of water about fifteen minutes; drain; add more water and boil two hours; just before taking up, add salt and pepper and half a pint of sweet cream.

STUFFED POTATOES.

Take a number of firm skin potatoes; clean well and bake them; when done, cut a piece off the end of each potato, scoop out as much of the inside as possible without breaking the skins, mash it with cream and butter and a little salt; add the whites of three eggs beaten to a stiff froth; fill up the skins with the paste and bake fifteen minutes.   MRS. A. HOFFMAN.

SUCCOTASH.

Good succotash wants tender young corn. Take six good-sized ears, and remove the kernels with a sharp knife; do not cut too deep, better not cut deep enough; then scrape; place over fire with water to cover and boil fifteen minutes. Have ready one pint of shelled lima beans, green; wash; cover with hot water; let them stand two or three minutes; drain, and add the beans to the corn; boil one-half hour, or till the beans are well cooked; season with butter, salt and pepper. A cupful of cream improves it.

SUMMER SQUASH.

Select the small crook-neck, those which are well grown but still tender enough to be penetrated by the thumb nail. Wash and put in a muslin bag; boil till done from one-half to three-fourths of an hour; squeeze and drain in the bag; turn out, and add salt, butter and pepper to taste. The seeds and skins are good at this stage of growth and they should never be cooked after the seeds are hard.

SWEET POTATOES.

Wash clean and place in a kettle of boiling hot water and let boil twenty minutes; take out and place in dripping-pan and bake in a quick oven till done. Or pare and slice; place them in a saucepan with a bit of butter, and sprinkle them with salt and barely cover them with water, covering them closely that they may steam quickly; when soft all through, add sweet cream or a little more butter; mash lightly, and they are ready to serve.

TOMATOES BAKED.

Pour boiling water over them and remove the skin ; cut them in small pieces; season with salt and pepper; put them in a pan with bread crumbs and pieces of butter; cover closely, and bake three-quarters of an hour. When done, mash, and serve hot.

TOMATOES RAW.

Do not loosen the skins with scalding water, as it destroys the crispness and flavor, but pare with a sharp knife; slice and lay in a glass dish; make a seasoning of vinegar, salt and pepper, stirring a piece of ice around in it. Pour it over the tomatoes; keep them ice cold until wanted.

TOMATOES STEWED.

Scald with boiling water and peel; put them in a saucepan; season with pepper, salt and butter; let them cook half or three-quarters of an hour. A tablespoonful of sugar can be added, while boiling, if desired.

TOMATO TOAST.

Scald and peel nice fresh tomatoes, and stew till tender; season with butter, pepper, salt and a little sugar. Take as many slices of bread as needed for your family ; toast nicely ; butter and arrange in a deep dish with some of the tomato on each slice; cover and serve at once.

TOMATOES WITH MACARONI.

Break one-half pound of macaroni in short pieces; cover with cold water and boil till tender—about three-fourths of an hour. Have ready one pint of ripe tomato stewed till tender; thicken with one heaping teaspoonful of flour rubbed smooth in a little water, and season with salt, pepper and two or three ounces of butter; boil this sauce up once, and pour over the macaroni, which has been drained and arranged in a suitable dish.

TURNIPS.

Wash, peel, cut in thin slices and put in kettle with water enough to cover; add a tablespoonful of sugar and boil until you can easily pierce them with a fork. Drain; mash fine; season with butter, pepper and salt.

WILTED LETTUCE.

Place in a vegetable dish lettuce that has been very carefully picked and washed each leaf by itself; cut across the dish four or five times, and sprinkle, with salt; add a cupful of good vinegar and pour it boiling hot over the lettuce; mix it well with a fork, and garnish with slices of hard boiled egg.

WINTER SQUASH.

Cut up; take out inside; put in the oven, and bake in the shell an hour; serve in the shell, or scrape out; mash; season with butter, pepper and salt; if too dry, add milk or cream.

Come, come; good wine is a good, familiar creature, if it be well used. —OTHELLO.

DOMESTIC WINES.

CURRANT WINE—No. 1.

One gallon of currant juice, two of soft water. To each gallon of this mixture, add four pounds of brown sugar. Let it stand and ferment a week or ten days. Keep a jug of the mixture to fill up the keg with so that it may run over when it works. When through working, put a pint of whisky in the keg. After it has stood in the cellar a month or two, bottle.

MRS. T. J. MARTIN.

CURRANT WINE (Black)—No. 2.

Put black currants into a jar and mash them ; pour boiling water over them until covered ; set in a cool place twenty-four hours. Strain this mixture through a coarse cloth as dry as possible. To one gallon of juice add four pounds of sugar. Put into a jug or keg and let it stand until done fermenting. Add one-half sheet of isinglass to every three gallons. Cork tight, and bottle at Christmas time. MRS. WAUGH.

CURRANT WINE—No. 3.

For ten gallons of wine, take thirty pounds of currants on the stems, thirty-five pounds of brown sugar, twenty-seven quarts of water; measure the water before commencing to mash the currants, and pour some over your hands to keep the juice cool; strain the juice through a hair sieve or strong cloth ; pour the juice and the rest of the water upon the sugar; stir it well and break all the lumps; let the wine stand in the tub twenty-four hours in a moderate heat; then put it in a barrel in the cellar. This quantity will produce sufficient to fill up the barrel, while it is fermenting. Keep the barrel open until the fermentation ceases and then fasten it up. To be bottled the same as grape wine.

Mrs. S. J. Yundt.

CURRANT WINE—No. 4.

Wash the currants. To one gallon of mashed currants add one of water. Let it stand three days in a stone jar; stir occasionally. Squeeze the juice and fruit through a bag as for jelly. To every gallon of juice add three pounds of "C" coffee sugar. Let this mixture stand in a jar for two or three days and skim whenever the scum rises to the top. Put it in a liquor keg and stand it in the shed until fall. Shake it up every day. Take it to the cellar for the winter, and after it has stood two or three months, bottle, if you choose. Mrs. B. Himmelsbach.

CHERRY BOUNCE.

Half bushel of wild cherries, pounded and put in cheese cloth bags, five gallons of brandy, whisky, or New England rum. Let it stand three months; add two gallons of water and five pounds of sugar. It will be fit for use in a week.

Miss Hattie Whitney,
Green Bay, Wis.

GRAPE WINE.

To every gallon of wine put three pounds and a half ($3\frac{1}{2}$) of sugar. To make ten gallons of wine, a large washtubful of grapes picked off the stems, which are to be well-mashed and squeezed, and then strained through a hair sieve to express all the juice. Mix the juice and sugar together, and measure it to see if it is ten gallons; if not, add more juice: or, failing in grapes, add water. An extra gallon is necessary to add in order to have ten gallons. Leave it in the tub in a moderate heat until fermentation has thoroughly commenced; then put it in the cask in the cellar with the bung out until fermentation ceases, when it is to be bunged up and left until the next spring, when it is to be drawn off and bottled. The extra gallon requires no more sugar. Brown sugar is to be used.

GOOSEBERRY WINE.

To each pound of ripe gooseberries allow one quart of water; bruise the gooseberries; then add the water; let it stand (after stirring well) for twelve or fourteen hours, then strain it; then add the sugar, as many pounds as you used quarts of water; let it stand two days; stir it often to dissolve sugar; put it into the barrel, allowing it to go through the process of fermenting, and fill up the barrel as with currant wine.

Mrs. S. J. Yundt.

MADEIRA WINE.

To ten gallons of water add thirty pounds of moist sugar; boil it half an hour and skim it clear; when quite cold, put to every gallon a quart of ale; let it stand to work two or three days in a tub; then put it in the barrel with one pound of brown sugar candy, six pounds of raisins, one quart of brandy and a little isinglass; when it has done working, stop it close and let it stand twelve months before bottling. N. B.—Be sure and not stop it down too soon.

Mrs. S. J. Yundt.

RAISIN WINE.

To one and one-fourth hundred-weight of raisins well picked and chopped, put eighteen gallons of water which has had six ounces of hops boiled in it for half an hour; let it stand until it is luke-warm, then put in your raisins; put it into a tub and let it work ten days stirring it well three or four times a day; then strain it off through a sieve and press your raisins thoroughly; turn it into your barrel; let it stand for four months; then add three pounds of sugar and one quart of brandy; let it stand six or eight months.

Miss Bowman,
New Orleans.

NOURISHING AND REFRESHING DRINKS.

CHOCOLATE.

Put one square of Baker's chocolate, two tablespoonfuls of sugar, two tablespoonfuls of hot water and a pinch of salt in a porcelain saucepan and boil until smooth; stir constantly; add, gradually, one pint of boiling water and one of hot milk. Use all milk and two squares of the chocolate, if you wish it richer.

Miss Lincoln.

CHOCOLATE (Mexican).

Two cupfuls of milk and the same of water. Place in a porcelain kettle or tin utensil for boiling; add the yolk of an egg beaten with two tablespoonfuls of sugar; let it come to a boil; then stir in half a cupful of Baker's chocolate, grated or scraped; let it boil until it separates. Beat the white of an egg to a stiff froth and, when you serve, place a little on the top of each cup.

Mrs. John A. McRea.

CLARET CUP.

Quarter of a bottle of claret, one pint of soda water, one lemon cut very thin, four tablespoonfuls of powdered sugar, quarter teaspoonful of grated nutmeg, half wineglassful of brandy, one wineglassful of sherry wine. Half an hour before use, put in a large piece of ice to make it perfectly cool.

Louise Smith,
Ottowa, Ont.

CREAM BEER.

Two ounces of tartaric acid, two pounds of white sugar, the juice of one lemon; add three pints of water, and boil five minutes; when nearly cold, add the whites of three eggs well beaten, with one-half cupful of flour, and one-half ounce of essence of wintergreen. Bottle and keep in a cool place. Take two tablespoonfuls of this mixture in a tumblerful of water, and add one-fourth teaspoonful of soda.

Mrs. J. E. Dickenson.

EGG NOGG.

Beat yolks and whites of six eggs; stir the yolks into a quart of rich milk or thin cream; add one-half pound of white sugar and a cupful of brandy or whisky; lastly, stir in the well beaten whites of the eggs.

If you wish to make an egg nogg for a sick person, beat up the yolk of one egg with a tablespoonful of sugar until it creams; put this in a tumbler and pour over it a tablespoonful of wine or brandy; fill up the tumbler with fresh milk and stir in the white of the egg beaten to a stiff froth. Pouring the wine or liquor on to the egg, cooks it and makes it more palatable for an invalid.   J. W. Squires.

NECTAR.

Six pounds of sugar, four ounces of tartaric acid, two quarts of water; put this in a porcelain kettle and heat slowly; just before it comes to a boil, take from the stove and stir in the whites of four well-beaten eggs; strain and cool and flavor with lemon or vanilla. Kept on the ice in summer, this makes a very refreshing beverage.   Mrs. Geo. C. Ginty.

POP.

Put two ounces of cream of tartar into a jar with the juice and peel of two lemons and a few pieces of ginger root; pour over them seven quarts of boiling water; when cool, strain through a gauze sieve; sweeten to taste, and add a large tablespoonful of fresh yeast; bottle and set by the fire all night. It will be fit for use next day.

RASPBERRY VINEGAR—No. 1.

Take a waterpailful of raspberries, turn them into a large stone crock and mash them; cover with good cider vinegar; place near the stove for one day. Squeeze this mixture through a bag, and to each quart of this juice add one pint of water and five pounds of the best white sugar. Heat slowly until the sugar dissolves, and then boil down until like syrup. Bottle while hot, and cover your corks with sealing mixture, so that it will be air tight. This is a very refreshing drink and particularly so to invalids or persons with a fever. When you use it, put two tablespoonfuls in a tumbler and fill up with ice-cold water.

MRS. GEO. C. GINTY.

RASPBERRY VINEGAR—No. 2.

To one quart of raspberries use one pint of vinegar. Let them stand twelve hours; then squeeze and strain. To one pint of juice take one pound of loaf sugar. Boil on a slow fire three-quarters of an hour. When cool, bottle and seal. Drink in summer, about a dessertspoonful to a glass of water. Very nice.

MRS. S. J. YUNDT.

Sweet, sweet, sweet poison for the age's tooth.

—KING JOHN.

CANDY.

These receipts are all good and have shortened many a winter's evening, and Sunday afternoon for restless boys and girls who must have something brewing in order to be happy. Be careful not to burn your candy, and do not cook your caramels until they are *brittle.* They should be well done, but soft.

BUTTER SCOTCH.

Three pounds of coffee A sugar, one-fourth pound of butter, one-half teaspoonful cream of tartar, eight drops of extract of lemon; add as much cold water as will dissolve the sugar ; boil without stirring until it hairs, or is brittle when dropped into cold water; when done, add the flavoring. Cool on buttered plates. If you pull this candy it will be *cream candy.* Half of this receipt is enough for ordinary occasions.

BUTTER TAFFY.

Two cupfuls of light brown sugar, one cupful of cold water, four tablespoonfuls of vinegar, two of molasses, one-half tablespoonful of butter. Cook without stirring until it spins to a thread or hairs when dropped from a spoon.

CREAM CANDY.

One pound of coffee A sugar and one cupful of water; boil over a very brisk fire. Try by dipping your finger and thumb first into cold water; then into the boiling sugar, and back into cold water quickly; when it will harden on your fingers it is done. Have ready a platter well-buttered; turn on this to cool, but never scrape out your kettle; when partly cool, add flavoring and beat with a knife as long as possible; then stir with your hands and form into a long roll and cut. Work quickly or it will grain.

Mrs. HERBERT BARKER.

CHOCOLATE CARAMELS—No. 1.

Two cupfuls of brown sugar, one of molasses, one of chocolate, a piece of butter the size of an egg, one table-spoonful of cream; boil eight minutes. Butter your tins, pour in the caramels, and set to cool. When nearly cold, cut in squares with a sharp knife.

Miss FANNY GINTY.

CHOCOLATE CARAMELS—No. 2.

One cupful of molasses, two cupfuls of light brown sugar, one cupful of milk or cream, a piece of butter the size of an egg, one-half pound of chocolate, three teaspoonfuls of vanilla; boil one-half hour. Put the vanilla in when it is almost done. Stir constantly.

V. M.

MAPLE CREAMS.

One-half as much water as maple sugar, cook without stirring, and when nearly done put in a small piece of butter; try it in water and when it begins to harden take off and stir rapidly until it becomes a waxen substance then roll in balls and put halves of English walnuts on either side.   Miss Louise Smith.

MOLASSES CANDY.

One quart of good molasses (not syrup), one-half cupful of vinegar, one cupful of sugar, butter size of an egg, one teaspoonful of saleratus; dissolve the sugar in the vinegar; pour into the molasses and boil, stirring frequently until it will harden when dropped into water; then stir in the butter and soda (the latter dissolved in warm water); flavor to taste; stir it up well and pour into buttered plates or tins.   As it cools, cut in squares for "taffy" or pull with the tips of the fingers until white, and cut in sticks.

     Marion Harland.

NUT TAFFY.

Four cupfuls of maple sugar; one-half pint of water or enough to dissolve the sugar; boil until it is brittle when dropped into water. Just before you take it from the fire add a tablespoonful of vinegar. Have hickory nut meats ready; lay them on a buttered dish and pour the taffy over them.

"OSCAR WILD" TAFFY.

Three pints of sugar first put in,
A shallow vessel made of tin,
Of vinegar add half a cup,
Of milk the same, then stir them up,
A little piece of butter, which

Will make your taffy taste quite rich.
Now put this compound on to boil,
(Don't stir it once, or it will spoil).
When done, a buttered tin will hold
The tempting mixture until cold ;
When hardened well, you then can send,
A dainty piece to tempt a friend.

YOUNG AMERICA.

SUGAR CANDY (Good for Little Folks).

Six cupfuls of sugar, one of vinegar, one of water, a tablespoonful of butter put in at the last with one teaspoonful of saleratus dissolved in warm water. Boil without stirring half an hour, or until it crisps in cold water; pull white; flavor to taste.

STICK CANDY.

To one pound of coffee "A" sugar, add one cupful of water, and one-half teaspoonful of cream of tartar; boil over a brisk fire, and try by dropping a spoonful in cold water; when brittle it is done. Do not stir while boiling, and do not scrape the kettle, or it will grain. Set where it will cool, and pull as long as possible. Form into sticks. Add flavoring while pulling.

MRS. HERBERT BARKER.

WALNUT CREAMS.

One cupful of walnuts chopped, two cupfuls of white sugar, one-half cupful of cold water; boil sugar and water without stirring, until it spins to a thread or hairs; flavor with vanilla. Set into cold water, and stir quickly until white. Then stir in the meats, and make into balls.

MRS. K. L. KENYON.

A King of shreds and patches.

—SHAKESPEARE.

MISCELLANEOUS.

A great many valuable receipts and useful hints will be found in this department. They come from the storehouses of our grandmothers, who found them in years of experience; as well as from the young, on the frontiers of progress, who are constantly bringing in new ideas to make "smooth the rough places."

One-fourth pound of white castile soap, four ounces of aqua ammonia, one ounce of ether, one ounce of alcohol; cut the soap in small bits and boil in one quart of water until dissolved; when cold, add four quarts more of water and the other ingredients. This is especially good for cleaning dress goods, men's clothing, spots on carpets, etc.

One pailful of boiling grease, six pailfuls of strong lye, five pailfuls of warm water; stir well every day for one week, and your soft soap is made.

Rub your zinc with kerosene. A little on a soft rag will make it look nicely.

Use vinegar and water to clean the mica windows of your coal stove.

A sure method to put out fire in pipes or chimneys: Wring an old piece of carpet out of cold water; roll round the stove pipe where it goes into the chimney; keep wetting (two or three times) and it will put the fire out.

French method of making fowl tender: After the fowl is stuffed and ready for the oven, roll it in a large sheet of soft paper; tie up closely with string; place in the oven one hour or half an hour, according to size; when it is thoroughly heated through, remove the paper and roast the fowl.

When you boil a ham do not boil it too long, but give it an hour in the oven after taking it from the pot It improves the flavor very much.

You can buy " Fruit Coloring " that will add greatly to fancy dishes, and it is perfectly harmless.

Little wire baskets are now sold to fry oysters, croquetts, etc., in.

A ricer is one of the necessary kitchen utensils of the age. Buy one and you will never regret it.

If you buy a double boiler you will wonder how you ever kept house without it.

Wipe off your carpets occasionally with ammonia and water. It brightens them up, and drives away moths.

Oxalic acid, dissolved in hot water, will clean paint from windows.

Stone jars that have become unfit for use from any cause, can be purified by filling with fresh earth and allowing it to remain two or three weeks.

Cotton batting is impervious to all life germs. Draw it carefully over a full jar of preserved fruit and it will prevent mould and fermentation.

Red and black ants may be effectually driven away by using Persian Insect Powder, sprinkled wherever they intrude.

A few trays of charcoal set in a damp cellar, will make the air pure and sweet, and if placed in a damp cellar where milk is kept, there will be no danger of the milk becoming tainted.

By placing a dish containing a good-sized lump of unslacked lime in a refrigerator the moisture will be absorbed, so removing all danger from mould.

Vinegar is better than ice for keeping fish. By putting a little vinegar on the fish it will keep perfectly well even in hot weather. Fish is often improved in flavor under this treatment.

To keep stockings from fading: Let them soak in hot salt and water until water is cold. Thoroughly rinse.

To keep ice for a sick room: Tie a square of coarse white flannel over a pitcher, leaving a cup-shaped depression of the flannel in the pitcher. Put broken ice in the flannel and cover it tightly with a thicker flannel. The ice will keep all night, and the water may be poured off as wanted.

A little pulverized charcoal will often sweeten a fowl that does not smell exactly sweet and yet is not bad. An onion placed in a fowl will do the same.

When you bake a fruit pie, wet a strip of white muslin and pin around the edge of the plate when you put it in the oven and it will not boil over.

When you wish a fine handkerchief to look like new after it is washed, wash it and while wet spread it out on a large pane of window glass; when dry, it will fall off and need no ironing.

Powdered alum will keep stove polish from burning off. Put in a little when you mix the polish.

To chop suet: Sprinkle flour over it while chopping and it will not adhere to the knife. Freeze it in the winter and you will have no trouble.

Mend lamps with melted alum. It is better than plaster of Paris.

Take a strip of muslin; hem it; sew buttons on one side and fasten your collars and cuffs on when you hang them out to dry after washing.

Half an ounce of ammonia, one of chloroform, half an ounce of oil of sassafras, one drachm of pulverized borax. Mix and shake well. Then add one gallon of deodorized gasoline. This makes cleansing fluid.

One pint of raw linseed oil, two ounces of spirits of wine, eight ounces of best cider vinegar, one ounce of butter of antimony, half an ounce of spirits of camphor, half an ounce of hartshorn. Rub on with old cotton flannel, and dry with the same. This is good furniture polish.

Silver polish: One pint of water, sixteen ounces of Paris white, one ounce of ammonia.

Tin polish: Sixteen ounces of pumice stone, fourteen ounces of muriatic acid, two pints of water.

Mirrors should not be hung where the sun shines upon them. It ruins them in a short time.

When you use gem tins and have not dough enough to fill every mold, fill the others with water.

Heat is a perfect disinfectant. If you have a pan, broiler, or any kitchen utensil that smells of fish, onions, etc., place the utensil in a hot oven for a few minutes after washing it and all odor will disappear.

To can fruit by use of salicylic acid: One-half ounce of salicylic acid; one pound of white sugar; one gallon of water. Mix acid and sugar together and dissolve with water. Put fruit in can or jar until full; then pour over the liquid, let settle one hour; then, if needed to cover fruit, pour over more liquid and cover closely from the air.

It is a great trouble sometimes to prepare suet for a
pudding when wanted.   You can keep it two or more
years by putting it in glass cans and pouring molasses
over it.   In the winter, flour will keep it.   Set your
bowl of suet in a corner of the flour bin, with flour
over it.

TABLE OF WEIGHTS AND MEASURES.

Four saltspoonfuls of liquid, - - One teaspoonful.
Four teaspoonfuls of liquid, - - One tablespoonful.
Three teaspoonfuls of dry material, - One tablespoonful.
Four tablespoonfuls of liquid, - - -
    One wine glassful, or one-half gill, or one-fourth cupful.
Two gills, - - - One cupful, or one-half pint.
Sixteen tablespoonfuls of liquid, - - One cupful.
Twelve tablespoonfuls dry material - - One cupful.
Eight heaping tablespoonfuls of dry material. - One cupful.
Four cupfuls of liquid, - - - - One quart.
Four cupfuls of flour, - - One pound, or one quart.
Two cupfuls of solid butter, - - - - One pound.
One-half cupful of butter, - - One-fourth pound.
Two cupfuls of granulated sugar, - - - One pound.
Two and one-half cupfuls of powdered sugar, - One pound.
Three cupfuls of meal, - - - One pound.
One pint of milk or water, - - - One pound.
One pint of chopped meat packed solidly, - One pound.
Nine large eggs, ten medium eggs, - - One pound.
One round tablespoonful of butter, - - One ounce.
One heaping tablespoonful of butter, - - -
    - - - - Two ounces, or one-fourth cupful.
Butter the size of an egg, - Two ounces, or one-fourth cupful.
One heaping tablespoonful of sugar, - - One ounce.
Two round tablespoonfuls of flour - - One ounce.
Two round tablespoonfuls of coffee, - - One ounce.
Two round tablespoonfuls of powdered sugar, - One ounce.
One tablespoonful of liquid, - - One-half ounce.
One bottle of brandy, - - - -
    One and one-half cupfuls, or twenty-four tablespoonfuls.
One small bottle Burnett's extract, - -
    - One-fourth cupful scant, or three tablespoonfuls.
One small bottle Burnett's extract, - Twelve teaspoonfuls.
One flask of olive oil, - - - -
    - One and one-third cupfuls, or twenty tablespoonfuls.

TABLE OF PROPORTIONS.

One scant measure of liquid to three full measures of flour, for bread.

One scant measure of liquid to two full measures of flour, for muffins.

One scant measure of liquid to one full measure of flour, for batters.

One-half cupful of yeast or one-fourth compressed yeast cake, to one pint of liquid.

One even teaspoonful of soda and two teaspoonfuls of cream of tartar to one quart of flour.

Three heaping or four even teaspoonfuls of baking powder to one quart of flour.

One teaspoonful of soda to one pint of sour milk.

One teaspoonful of soda to one cupful of molasses.

One saltspoonful of salt to one quart of milk for custards.

One teaspoonful of extract to one quart of custard.

One saltspoonful of salt to one loaf of sponge cake.

One teaspoonful of extract to one loaf of plain cake.

One saltspoonful of spice to one loaf of plain cake.

One teaspoonful of salt to one quart of soup stock, or two quarts of flour.

One saltspoonful of white pepper to one quart of soup stock.

One teaspoonful of mixed herbs to one quart of soup stock.

One tablespoonful of each chopped vegetable to one quart of soup stock.

A speck of cayenne pepper is what you can take up on the point of a pen-knife or on a quarter inch square surface.

A pinch of salt or spice is about a saltspoonful.

A pinch of hops is one-fourth of a cupful.

INDEX.

YEAST, BREAD, ROLLS, GEMS, ETC.

GRIDDLE CAKES, FRITTERS AND MUSH.

FROSTINGS AND FILLINGS.

GINGER CAKES AND COOKIES.

SUGAR COOKIES.

DOUGHNUTS AND FRIED CAKES.

PUDDINGS AND SAUCES.

PUDDING SAUCES.

ICE CREAM, ICES, CREAMS, CUSTARDS, JELLIES.

PIES.

PICKLES.

CATCHUPS AND SAUCES FOR MEATS, FISH AND VEGETABLES.

SALADS AND SALAD DRESSINGS.

SALAD DRESSINGS.

RELISHES AND HINTS FOR THE TABLE.

SOUPS.

FRESH FISH, SALT FISH, OYSTERS, ETC.

MEATS AND POULTRY.

TABLE:

Showing the proper Vegetables to serve with Meats, Game, Poultry, Fish, Etc...................................... 257

VEGETABLES.

DOMESTIC WINES.

NOURISHING AND REFRESHING DRINKS.

CANDY.

MISCELLANEOUS.

www.ingramcontent.com/pod-product-compliance
Lightning Source LLC
Chambersburg PA
CBHW021215270326
41929CB00010B/1145